Rutherford County in the Korean War

Rutherford County in the Korean War

Anita Price Davis and James M. Walker

Charleston London
the History PRESS

Published by The History Press
Charleston, SC 29403
www.historypress.net

Cover Images: Corporal Franks (second from left) stands in front of an M-4 Sherman tank while he attended the Armored School, Fort Knox, Kentucky. Franks trained as a tracked vehicle mechanic. Bobby Earl Franks died on June 29, 1969. *Courtesy of Shane Franks Atchley.*
Robert Boyce Harrill recalls that on board the *Tanner* there was a stoaway: a dog! The crew named the visitor "Stow," short for Stowaway. The men hid the animal and passed it from hand to hand when inspections were imminent. For his services Robert Boyce Harrill earned, among others, the National Defense Service Medal and the Good Conduct Medal. *Courtesy of Robert Boyce Harrill.*

First published 2006

Manufactured in the United Kingdom

ISBN 1.59629.109.5

Library of Congress Cataloging-in-Publication Data

Davis, Anita Price.
Rutherford County in the Korean War / Anita Price Davis and James M.
Walker.
p. cm.
ISBN 1-59629-109-5 (alk. paper)
1. Korean War, 1950-1953--Participation, American. 2. Soldiers--North
Carolina--Rutherford County--Biography. 3. Soldiers--North
Carolina--Rutherford County--Biography--Pictorial works. 4. Rutherford
County (N.C.)--Biography. 5. Rutherford County (N.C.)--Biography--Pictorial
works. I. Walker, James M. II. Title.
DS919.D38 2006
951.904'23756913--dc22

2006007438

Contents

Preface

The Korean War would cost the Democratic People's Republic of Korea (DPRK) and its Chinese allies. They would suffer approximately 600,000 casualties. The People's Republic of China suffered approximately 900,000 casualties.

The Republic of Korea suffered 415,004 killed and 428,568 missing and wounded.

During the Korean War, the United States suffered 106,978 wounded or missing in action (MIA). The total dead was 54,246; the casualties, therefore, were 161,224. Rutherford County lost 13 of its sons and brothers. *Rutherford County in the Korean War* honors the Rutherford County men and women who served, those at the home front, and particularly those who made the supreme sacrifice:

Frank Robert Barrett
Lolan O. Bridges
Cameron M. Flack
Roy S. Flynn Jr.
Clarence W. Gee
Homer Green
A.C. Greene
Fred E. Guffey
Martin A. Lawing
John B. Ledbetter
James H. Lowrance
Bryant Womack
Thomas W. Yelton

Bill Ingram (Cliffside) remembers his early dreams of joining the United States Navy. Bill wrote this poem about his dreams for the future and gave permission for the authors to share his poem with others—especially those who also have dreams.

The Dreamer—1945
Bill Ingram

On his back, eyes watching the cumulus form,
shapes of things that usually precede a storm.
"What is this?" he said as ships came into view.
Ships belong down here in a sea of ocean blue.

Battleships and Destroyers, they cannot fly,
across this universe and otherwise azure sky.
Look how slowly and carefully they creep,
searching for a port and harbor that's deep.

"I will close my eyes until they are gone," said he,
but still they remained for the young boy to see.
This has to be a mirage, the boy then surmised,
but shortly thereafter, popped up another fleet of five.

The cumulus turned into gray warships of two,
for the lad who dreamed of wearing the blue.
Magellan, Cook, and Perry, all heroes of the deep,
would remain in his mind forever even in his sleep.

He dreamed of the ladies who would welcome him so,
on paradise islands with their absence of snow.
They appeared before him swaying with flair,
though troubled by puberty, he didn't dare.

Bill Ingram realized his dreams. This book, *Rutherford County in the Korean War*, includes more information about Bill Ingram and his family.

Introduction

Rutherford County had served sacrificially in defeating Nazi Germany and the Japanese Empire during World War II. Returning soldiers were putting the past behind them and preparing for a brighter future.

Most were glad the Japanese had surrendered. Some had been preparing for immediate engagement. In fact, James Grady Willis Sr. was actually on board a ship en route to the Pacific theater when the surrender occurred. Private First Class James Grady Willis Sr., Company A, 342nd Infantry Regiment, 86th Infantry Division, had served as a truck driver for his unit during the Central European Campaign in World War II. Willis was one of many men who thought they would have to serve against Japan, but with the surrender of Japan in August of 1945, he and his fellow comrades were able to return to duty and discharge in the United States. Willis's decorations include the American Theater Campaign Medal, the European-African-Middle Eastern (EAME) Campaign Medal with Bronze Service Star, Sharpshooter with the M1 carbine, the Asiatic Pacific Campaign Medal, the Good Conduct Medal and the World War II Victory Medal; Willis was a highly qualified driver and earned the Driver and Mechanical Badge.

Typical of those who served in World War II are Wilbur G. Martin and his brother David C. Martin. After their return to the county, they assumed jobs in local textile mills, Florence and Fieldcrest.

Technician Fifth Grade Wilbur G. Martin had served in the Northern Apennines, the Ardennes and the Rhineland. He had served there as a truck driver who hauled bombs for the 452nd Bomb Squadron, the Ninth Air Force. He called his truck "the Paper Doll."

Wilbur had earned the Good Conduct Medal, the EAME Campaign Medal with three Bronze Service Stars and the World War II Victory Medal.

Technician Fifth Grade David C. Martin had served in the 115th Chemical Processing Company as a cook. While serving in Northern France and the Rhineland, he received the Good Conduct

Medal, the EAME Campaign Medal with two Bronze Service Stars and qualified as a marksman on the .30-caliber rifle M1.

Herbert Morgan Walker of Ellenboro was drafted into the United States Army in 1946. Walker represents all those who served between the end of World War II and the Korean War. Attaining the rank of corporal, Walker served with Company D, 342nd Infantry Regiment, 86th Infantry Division in the Pacific theater. Corporal Walker served as a guard patrolman; he guarded Japanese prisoners of war and trained Filipino scouts. Walker received transfer in 1950 to the European theater of operations where he was a communications chief in Company M, 351st Infantry Regiment, 88th Division. At the outbreak of the Korean War, Walker's unit was tasked with patrolling the Yugoslavian border while on high alert because of "East European Communist hostility." Corporal Walker earned the Good Conduct Medal, World War II Victory Medal, Army of Occupation with Germany clasp, National Defense Service Medal, Honorable Discharge Lapel Pin and Marksman Badge (Rifle). Walker enjoys the story of his train ride from Cincinnati to Petersburg, Virginia, on the Norfolk and Western Railway with a friend from West Virginia; after enjoying a wonderful dining car dinner, the steward placed a round bowl of water at each table setting. Herbert, unsure of the purpose of the water, turned to watch the other diners to see the protocol. When Walker looked back at his companion, his friend had consumed his bowl of water.

William Garth Harrill, a native of Rutherford County, participated in the occupation of Berlin after World War II. William Garth Harrill was the brother of Rebecca Jane Harrill (Thompson) from the Forest City area. His parents were Selma Jane Price (Harrill) and Clark Miles Harrill. The Harrill/Price/Thompson families were very much involved in the service of their country. His relatives Keith Price and Robert Benjamin Thompson also served their country; they are discussed later in this book.

Corporal Herbert Morgan Walker in 1950 served in the European theater of operations where he was a communications chief in Company M, 351st Infantry Regiment, 88th Division. *Courtesy of Herbert Morgan Martin.*

Technician Fifth Grade Wilbur G. Martin (left) stands with his friend Bates and his truck that he named "The Paper Doll," after a popular song. *Courtesy of Wilbur G. Martin.*

This is a formal portrait of Technician Fifth Grade Wilbur G. Martin during his World War II service. *Courtesy of Wilbur G. Martin.*

Private First Class James Grady Willis Sr. was on a ship en route to Japan when World War II ended. *Courtesy of Teresa Hopler.*

Technician Fifth Grade David C. Martin, like his brother Wilbur G. Martin, served during World War II. *Courtesy of Wilbur G. Martin and Ronnie Martin, David's grandson.*

Prologue to the Korean War

The Korean War had its beginnings at the end of World War II. The Soviet Union and the United States agreed to temporary occupation zones divided by the thirty-eighth north parallel. The area south of the thirty-eighth parallel became the United States-supported Republic of Korea (ROK) on August 15, 1948. On September 9, 1948, the northern occupation zone became the Soviet-supported Democratic People's Republic of Korea (DPRK).

Japan had occupied Korea for forty years. The Soviet Union had invaded the northern portion of the Korean Peninsula and had occupied it since August of 1945; this move reflected their agreement to enter the war against Japan. The Soviet Union withdrew to the northern half of the peninsula upon the conclusion of World War II and the agreement between the United States and the Soviet Union.

The Communist Party with the support of the Soviet Union established a government in the northern portion of the country in the city of Pyongyang under the leadership of dedicated Communist Kim Il Sung. Kim had spent World War II inside the Soviet Union in preparation for his role as leader. The Republic of Korea established a democratic government in the south; its capital was at Seoul, and its president (elected on May 10, 1948) was Syngman Rhee, a professed Christian. Rhee had strong anti-Communist views, governed in an authoritarian manner and allowed internal security forces to detain and rigorously interrogate suspected Communist agents.

For five years both the north and the south struggled to establish working governments. The United States had supplied military advisors to work with the Republic of Korea. In June of 1949 the military forces of the United States withdrew except for an advisory group of five hundred soldiers. The two nations continued their belligerent posturing with each other.

On Sunday, June 25, 1950, at 4:00 p.m., 135,000 troops of the Democratic Republic of Korea (North Korea) attacked the south across the thirty-eighth parallel without warning.

The North Korean objective was the capture of Seoul and the destruction of the army of the Republic of Korea.

Serving in 1950 in Japan with the United States Air Force at the Itazuke Air Base was Sergeant George W. Roberson. Roberson recalls that on June 25, 1950, he was playing a round of golf for his base golf team at the Fifth Air Force Annual Golf Tournament at Koganei Golf Club in Tokyo, Japan, when the aggression occurred. After service in Japan, Roberson received assignment to Maxwell Air Force Base in Alabama in the Headquarters 3801st Maintenance and Supply Group. Upon his discharge in 1952, Roberson earned the Good Conduct Medal, the Army of Occupation Medal (Japan), the Korean Service Medal with three Bronze Service Stars, Republic of Korea Presidential Unit Citation and United Nations Service Medal.

On June 25, 1950, Sergeant George W. Roberson was playing a round of golf for his base golf team at the Fifth Air Force Annual Golf Tournament at Koganei Golf Club in Tokyo, Japan, when the aggression occurred. *Courtesy of George W. Roberson.*

Captain William Garth Harrill was the youngest company commander in the occupation of Berlin after World War II. His promotion was accompanied by a photo and a written citation. *Courtesy of Jane Thompson Gurley and Rebecca Jane Harrill Thompson.*

The Invasion by North Korea

JUNE 25, 1950–SEPTEMBER 14, 1950

President Harry S. Truman referred this case of naked aggression to the United Nations Security Council. Later on the same day—as invasion continued—the United Nations passed two resolutions: one to cease hostilities and the other authorizing the use of any necessary force in order to return the situation to status quo. A major reason that the resolutions passed was because the Soviet government was boycotting the Security Council at that time; they, therefore, could not veto the action. On June 27, 1950, from Washington, D.C., President Truman issued this statement: "We know that what is at stake is nothing less than our national security and the peace of the world," reports Max Hastings in *Korea*.

By June 28, 1950, the North Koreans had captured Seoul and had crossed the Han River, just outside Seoul. The five hundred American advisers had to retreat.

The only American forces available were in Japan and were under the command of General Douglas MacArthur. These troops were the First Cavalry Division, Seventh, Twenty-fourth and Twenty-fifth Infantry Divisions. Portions of these units were deployed to Pusan, South Korea, to contain the fighting. Many of the boys would write home that "You could smell Korea a long time before you ever saw it." None of these divisions were fully combat effective because of occupation duties in Japan. On June 30, 1950, President Truman had authorized the use of the U.S. Air Force and the U.S. Navy to interdict the North Korean advance.

The arriving troops in Pusan rushed north on July 5, 1950, to Osan. This delaying action was to gain time until the arrival of additional reinforcements authorized by General MacArthur.

By July 20, all four divisions held posts along the line of the Kum River near Taejon. Lieutenant General Walton H. Walker was in command of the troops of the Eighth Army, which would eventually include troops from the United Kingdom, Turkey, Philippines, New Zealand, Australia, Canada, France, Greece and others. Under North Korean pressure, however, the

Eighth Army had to retreat to the southeast. There they established a perimeter around the port of Pusan and held it into September of 1950.

Meanwhile General MacArthur had been planning for an amphibious landing on the west coast of Korea at Inchon (which is on the Yellow Sea twenty-five miles from Seoul) for a specific date: September 15, 1950. September 15 was one of only three possible dates that landing ship tanks (LSTs), which have a draft of twenty-nine feet, could come ashore during a three-hour period of high tide. Hastings writes that MacArthur had declared, "We must act now, or we will die…We shall land at Inchon, and I shall crush them." This assault would prove to be one of MacArthur's masterstrokes—a last, great victory.

During September the tide at Inchon can fall more than thirty-two feet twice a day. Later, most "Monday Morning Quarterbacks" considered MacArthur's assault to be insane—not only because of the combat involved but also because of the wide variance between low and high tide.

The Flack family (particularly Cameron, Mike and Charles and first cousin Austin D. Flack from Union Mills) were patriotic people who had done and were doing their part for their country. Master Sergeant Austin Devault Flack was a career soldier and was present at Schofield Barracks on the island of Oahu on December 7, 1941. Master Sergeant Flack also saw combat during the Korean War. He served as the battalion sergeant major. Flack's unit (Headquarters Battery, Sixty-third Field Artillery Battalion, Twenty-fourth Infantry Division) had entered Korea through the port at Pusan during the first week of the war (June 1950). During the desperate effort to "trade space for time," Sergeant Flack's battalion was overrun at Kongju-Songyo-Ri on July 14, 1950, barely three weeks into the Korean War.

Master Sergeant Flack's captivity began with a death march, writes Kasey C. Wilson in the July 24, 1998 issue of the *U.S. Soldiers' and Airmen's Home Newspaper*. "They marched us by night and hid us by day" so American troops would not detect us. "They did fix us a rice ball now and then, but sometimes we went for three days without a bite." On Halloween evening in 1950, "a brutal North Korean known as 'The Tiger' took command of our group. With the addition of civilian captives from the Salvation Army and the Red Cross there were close to 900 of us being held…The Tiger [who was in his thirties and had the coldest eyes you had ever seen]…picked out First Lieutenant Cordus H. Thornton and brought him up front and center and shot him in the head. I was no more than 30 feet away." All the captives had to turn in their dog tags. During one forced march in November, the North Koreans shot twenty-seven men who could not keep up.

In the January 1997 issue of *Reader's Digest* there is a story ("Johnson's List") about Tiger survivors; Tiger survivor Wayne "Johnnie" Johnson managed to keep a list of 496 men who had died in captivity and to bring the list home. Leaving school at an early age to enlist in the U.S. Army was Private Vernon D. Stallings, Twenty-first Infantry Regiment, Twenty-fourth Division; Stalling's friends Ed W. Scruggs and Malcolm McConnell recall that Stallings was a Tiger survivor along with fellow Rutherford County resident Austin D. Flack. Upon repatriation in August of 1953, only 262 of Tiger's captives were still alive.

Corporal Joseph E. Ford served with Battery B, Fifteenth Field Artillery Battalion, Second Infantry Division ("Warrior Division"). This Rutherford County soldier had enlisted at the age of seventeen and entered Korea on July 31, 1950, at Pusan. Ford served as a cannoneer on a 105-millimeter howitzer and provided fire support for U.S. and ROK troops.

By February 13, 1951, Corporal Joseph E. Ford's battery was in North Korea. Ford recalls the snow of that day. Ford would remain a POW in a North Korean camp near the Yalu River for the next two and a half years. Their treatment was without compassion and with no humanity. Ford recalls, "Men died by starvation, pneumonia, typhoid and malaria." Ford remembers that the guards gave the prisoners copies of the Communist Party's *Daily Worker* and the *Shanghai News*. Ford's release did not occur until August 13, 1953.

The Second Infantry Division was the first unit to receive a critical new support element: a Korean Augmentation to the United States Army. These Korean soldiers, known as KATUSAs, helped turn the tide for the American forces. (Even at the date of this writing, 2006, Korean soldiers remain part of the Second Infantry Division. In the year 2002, for example, 1,400 KATUSAs were serving.)

Robert "Bob" Humphries, U.S. Army medic, entered Korea at the Inchon invasion. By November 28, 1950, Humphries and other members of his unit had advanced north to the Chosin Reservoir. It was at this location that Chinese Communist Forces (CCF) forces shot up his jeep. Humphries saw the windshield shatter, and he fell out of the vehicle. When the jeep ran over his leg, Humphries was captured. Humphries attributed his survival to "growing up in poverty"; he believed that many of the men who died simply gave up hope.

Corporal Bailey Gillespie entered service in 1948 at the age of eighteen. Gillespie was part of Company C, the Twenty-seventh Infantry Regiment ("Wolfhounds"), Twenty-fifth Infantry Division ("Tropical Lightning"); this division would remain in combat for thirty-seven months. (The unit would later receive two Korean Presidential Unit Citations and would participate in all ten Korean War campaigns.) Gillespie entered Korea when his unit deployed from Japan to serve under Lieutenant General Walton H. Walker. Corporal Gillespie's unit participated in the fighting withdrawal of U.S. forces attempting to impede the North Korean advance toward Pusan. At their location in the area around Taegu, the Wolfhounds served as General Walker's fire brigade and helped prevent a North Korean breakthrough of the city of Pusan. In tending the wounded, Bailey saw the injury and death of many of his friends and comrades.

After MacArthur's Inchon invasion, the Twenty-fifth Infantry Division advanced through Seoul and Pyongyang. After a Thanksgiving meal, the advance continued until CCF forces attacked the UN units.

The CCF forces had taken hundreds of American and Allied prisoners. The enemy troops immediately began to march the captured POWs to camps near the Chinese border. Bailey recalls that during the ten-day forced march, the enemy only fed them twice and he was butt-stroked in the back with a rifle during the march; he still suffers muscle pain from the blow. Gillespie remembers captive Captain Sidney Esensten, U.S. Army physician from Minneapolis, Minnesota. Esensten was a patriotic inspiration to the sick and wounded in the North Korean POW camp. Their life was hard. The men slept on the floor in the huts. Most of the captured were without winter uniforms; many had lost their shoes, and gangrene was beginning to set in at their wounds. Lice infestation posed a constant misery. Typhus, typhoid and pneumonia were constant companions. The men were in "the care of those who did not care if they lived or died."

The men who died remained stacked like cordwood because the ground was too hard to bury them during the winter. Partially cooked grain was their staple twice a day, but there was never enough to curb the hunger pains. The winter temperatures could drop to minus forty degrees Fahrenheit and below. The prisoners maintained their spirits only through their faith in a higher power; Bailey treasured his Testament and shared it with others who read aloud. Later, night blindness from malnutrition prevented their reading aloud. This was Bailey's life for over three years.

Sergeant Lolan Odell Bridges, Headquarters and Headquarters Company, Thirty-first Infantry Regiment, Seventh Infantry Division, had served throughout World War II. He was one of the first Rutherford County soldiers sent to Korea. On December 2, 1950, the United States Army declared Sergeant Bridges missing in action in North Korea. *Courtesy of Dorothy Haynes Dixon.*

On July 14, 1950, Master Sergeant Austin Flack was the first person from the county to be captured in the Korean War; he was held captive 1,143 days before his release on August 19, 1953. *Courtesy of Joseph E. Ford.*

Corporal Joseph E. Ford served with Battery B, Fifteenth Field Artillery Battalion, Second Infantry Division ("Warrior Division"). Ford's unit, after helping to hold the Pusan perimeter, advanced north to the thirty-eighth parallel after the successful invasion at Inchon on September 15, 1950. *Courtesy of Joseph E. Ford.*

On February 13, 1951, North Korean and Chinese Communist troops overran Joseph E. Ford's unit and two Republic of Korea (ROK) divisions. *Courtesy of Joseph E. Ford.*

Corporal Bailey Gillespie and other members of the medical detachment moved to set up an aid station on November 27, 1950. Enemy forces captured Corporal Gillespie and some other members of the medical detachment. *Courtesy of Bailey Gillespie.*

Sergeant George Adam Moore Jr. enlisted in the U.S. Marine Corps in 1948. He received training as a clerk/typist, completed personal administration courses at Parris Island, South Carolina, did a tour in Korea and served until 1969. He earned the Commendation Medal (U.S. Navy), Good Conduct Medal with silver/bronze star (which means during his career he received the Good Conduct Medal on six occasions), National Defense Service Medal, Korean Service Medal, Vietnam Service Medal, Combat Action Ribbons, Republic of Korea Presidential Unit Citation, Republic of Vietnam Meritorious Unit Citation (two times), Republic of Vietnam Campaign Medal with Device (1960), Marine Corps Expert Rifle and Marine Corps Expert Pistol. *Courtesy of Lois Morgan Moore.*

Corporal Elbert Munsey enlisted in the United States Army five days after his seventeenth birthday. He served in the Medical Detachment, Forty-fourth Engineer Construction Battalion, Thirty-eighth Infantry Regiment, Second Infantry Division. The Forty-fourth Engineer Construction Battalion helped build bridges over the Han River for the northern advance; he still recalls the devastated North Korean villages as the unit advanced. The Red Chinese counter-attack brought the retreat of troops south of the thirty-eighth parallel. Munsey earned the Combat Medical Badge, the Korean Service Medal with five Bronze Service Stars, the ROK Presidential Unit Citation and the Meritorious Unit Commendation. *Courtesy of Elbert Munsey.*

Sgt. Sylvester Antolak was a converted VC2-S-AP-2 type ship built under a maritime commission contract, on May 3, 1945. Its name came from a World War II Medal of Honor recipient. Sergeant Antolak's citation reads in part that he "was directly responsible for eliminating 20 Germans, capturing an enemy machine gun, and clearing the path for his company to advance." Corporal Elbert Munsey was one of the troops shuttled aboard. *Courtesy of Elbert Munsey.*

World War II veteran Grover C. Haynes had entered Clemson University after World War II. To supplement his wife June's and his income, Grover joined the Navy Reserves. After his 1950 graduation, they were living in Denver, Colorado, when Haynes received his recall. Haynes served aboard USS *Briarius* for sixteen months. Grover's sense of humor emerged with his closing remark: "Not much of a story, is it?" *Courtesy of Grover C. Haynes.*

United States Army medic Robert "Bob" Humphries entered Korea at the Inchon invasion. At the Chosin Reservoir on November 28, 1950, Chinese Communist Forces captured Robert. He would spend 997 days in captivity. *Courtesy of Ray Humphries and the* Gastonia Gazette.

Drive to the Yalu

SEPTEMBER 15, 1950–NOVEMBER 27, 1950

Following the successful invasion at Inchon and the race north from the Pusan perimeter, the United States and United Nations Command Forces reached the thirty-eighth parallel following the liberation of Seoul on September 27, 1950. The optimistic prediction at this time was that the troops would be home by Christmas. The Allied troops began a push into North Korean territory. The Chinese Communist government threatened intervention if troops of the United States and United Nations crossed north of the thirty-eighth parallel. General Douglas MacArthur refused to heed the Chinese warning and allowed the advance to continue. The UN forces took the North Korean capital of Pyongyang on October 19, 1950.

On October 26, ROK forces reached the Yalu River. Chinese Communist Forces counterattacked. Within one month, no less than three hundred thousand Communist troops had entered the war.

Meanwhile on the east coast, US X Corps, including the Seventh Infantry Division, reached the Yalu on November 20, 1950. By November 27, the CCF had surrounded UN forces at the Chosin Reservoir.

Sergeant Lox Eugene Ayers enlisted in the United States Army at the age of eighteen for a period of three years. Ayers served with Company L, Third Battalion, Thirty-first Regiment ("Polar Bears"), Seventh Division ("Bayonet"). He participated in the drive from the thirty-eighth parallel to the Chosin Reservoir in North Korea. Ayers remembers vividly the minus-thirty-degree Fahrenheit temperatures in the middle of November in 1950. During this drive Ayers suffered shrapnel wounds on December 1, 1950.

The understrengthed Seventh Division, to which Sergeant Ayers belonged, integrated eight thousand ROK soldiers to augment its power. Each Seventh Division soldier received a Korean "buddy" or KATUSA for training and combat. Sergeant Lox Eugene Ayers recalls the KATUSAs and other events of the war. He earned the Purple Heart Medal, Combat Infantryman's Badge, Army of Occupation Medal (Japan) and the Korean Service Medal with three Bronze Service Stars.

In late December of 1950 after brutal fighting and frigid temperatures, the UN forces withdrew. MacArthur's wish to have the troops home by Christmas was to be unfulfilled.

Ralph Leonard Dixon enlisted in the United States Army on June 7, 1949. He received basic training at Fort Jackson in Columbia, South Carolina, and served fourteen months in Korea with Battery A, Ninth Field Artillery Battalion, which was attached to the Third Infantry Division ("Rock of the Marne"). His service with the 155-millimeter howitzers permanently affected his hearing. *Courtesy of Ralph and Dorothy Haynes Dixon.*

Staff Sergeant Ralph Leonard Dixon married Dorothy Haynes Dixon on November 9, 1951, at the parsonage of the Cliffside Baptist Church. Pastor Tom S. Lawrence performed the ceremony. Lolan Odell Bridges (mentioned earlier as missing in action) was the uncle of Dorothy Haynes Dixon. Sergeant Dixon qualified as a Rifle Sharpshooter and earned, among others, the Korean Service Medal and the Good Conduct Medal. *Courtesy of Ralph and Dorothy Haynes Dixon.*

At the Veterans Day Luncheon on November 11, 2005, Sergeant Lox Eugene Ayers displays this treasured silkscreen with his image and that of his friend Sergeant Erwin Crews; Crews died as a result of the attack at Chosin Reservoir. Ayers suffered shrapnel wounds there on December 1, 1950. *Courtesy of James M. Walker and Lox Eugene Ayers.*

William Harrill "Bill" Withrow was at the Naval Academy from 1937 through February of 1941 before receiving his commission as ensign. He served aboard the USS *Wasp* in World War II until it sank on September 15, 1942. He had flight training in New Orleans in 1942 and seaplane training at Naval Air Station in Pensacola and Jacksonville; he had other duty at Whitby Island Naval Air Station near Seattle. During the Korean War he served upon aircraft carriers from the Aleutian Islands (North Pacific) to New Zealand (South Pacific). Withrow retired from the United States Navy with a rank of commander after twenty-nine years, six months and a half-day of service. *Courtesy of William Harrill "Bill" Withrow.*

Private Hugh G. Brooks, son of Rosa Lee and George Ervin Brooks of Rutherford County, served in the United States Army during the Korean War. *Courtesy of Sara Brooks.*

Sergeant Douglas Dean White, USMC, First Marine Division, remembers standing honor guard to General Douglas MacArthur when MacArthur left Japan. *Courtesy of Frances Silver.*

Sergeant Douglas Dean White qualified as a Rifle Sharpshooter. During his active service in Korea (1951–53) Sergeant White served with a thirteen-man sniper team. This image shows him with his sniper rifle. Later he served as a military policeman. For his services Sergeant White received the Good Conduct Medal, the Korean Service Medal, the United Nations Service Medal, the National Defense Service Medal and others. *Courtesy of Frances Silver.*

Private Hugh Brooks successfully completed not only his paratrooper training but also his entire term of service. Upon his discharge on February 15, 1952, his records indicated "Excellent character, excellent efficiency, and favorable consideration for the Good Conduct Medal." Hugh and his wife Sara Gertrude Smith had a successful family life also. They had five children: Linda, Steven, Cheryl, William and Gail. *Courtesy of Sara Brooks.*

The Chinese Intervene and UN Counteroffensive

NOVEMBER 28, 1950–APRIL 21, 1951

With the withdrawal of UN forces below the thirty-eighth parallel, General Walton H. Walker redeployed the Eighth Army and additional forces across the peninsula where he began to develop a coast-to-coast defense line. The X Corps with the First Marine Division and the Seventh Division retired from the Chosin Reservoir through bitter fighting to Hungnam, a city on the east coast. The troops then evacuated the city by sea and proceeded to Pusan, where they would become part of the Eighth Army. This retrograde movement was completed by Christmas Eve 1950. Unfortunately, the Eighth Army Commander Lieutenant General Walton H. Walker had been killed in a jeep on an ice-covered road on December 23, 1950.

With Walker's death, General MacArthur replaced Eighth Army Commander Lieutenant General Walton H. Walker with Lieutenant General Matthew Bunker Ridgway. Ridgway found the Eighth Army to be dispirited because of the arduous battles in the north and the humiliating withdrawals that had been necessary because of the overwhelming number of Chinese forces. By the last day of 1950, Communist forces numbered half a million and were increasing. Ridgway himself found the defensive line to be weak and thin. His plan for defense was twofold: to improve morale by working through corps and division commanders and to move reinforcements and reserves to threatened sections of the line.

Communist forces opened their attacks toward Seoul on New Year's Eve 1951. By January 4, 1951, the UN forces had pulled out of Seoul, and the CCF troops entered the city. Ridgway's operational plan was to keep the enemy from further advances and to inflict maximum casualties on the enemy with minimal casualties to UN troops.

MacArthur was not sanguine that Ridgway could hold his position on the peninsula. He proposed bringing major reinforcements to the area, blockading the Chinese coast, destroying Chinese industries with attacks from the air and sea, reinforcing UN troops with Chinese Nationalist forces and allowing diversionary operations on the Chinese mainland by Chinese Nationalist troops. Officials in Washington, D.C., declined to approve MacArthur's proposals. The Truman administration advocated a policy of confining the fighting to the Korean peninsula.

During these high-level discussions among the Allied leadership, Ridgway's revitalized and rejuvenated Eighth Army had thwarted CCF forces. By mid-March 1951 the Eighth Army and UN forces had once more recaptured Seoul and now stood at the thirty-eighth parallel.

Serving in the United States Navy during 1950–54 was Utilityman Third Class Roger Evarts. He served as a plumber and mechanic in the Seabees MCB #1. Evarts served in Newfoundland, Canada, in French Morocco at Port Lyautey, and in Cuba at Port Guantanamo Naval Base. For his services, Rutherford County native Evarts earned the Good Conduct Medal and the National Defense Service Medal. *Courtesy of Roger Evarts.*

Private First Class Robert Bouldin, Military Police Detachment, Section 1, 1447 SCU, entered service for the first time on September 25, 1942. Bouldin served in Normandy, Northern France and Rhineland as a truck driver. For his services in World War II, he earned the Combat Infantryman's Badge, along with the EAME Campaign Medal with three Bronze Service Stars. *Courtesy of Mary Bouldin.*

Upon discharge, Robert Bouldin worked for four years with Yellow Cab in Gastonia, North Carolina. He re-enlisted in January of 1949 and served with the Headquarters and Headquarters Company of the Twenty-eighth Infantry, Eighth Infantry Division. For his Korean War service, Bouldin earned his second Combat Infantryman's Badge with the Headquarters of the Fifth Regimental Combat Team, the Korean Service Medal with three Bronze Service Stars and the United Nations Service Medal. *Courtesy of Mary Bouldin.*

After his second tour of duty, Robert and Mary E. Bouldin were married on March 24, 1952. This thirty-sixth anniversary photograph attests to their long and happy marriage. Robert died on January 21, 1998. *Courtesy of Mary Bouldin.*

Airman Second Class Harry A. Ingram Jr. of Cliffside enlisted on May 29, 1950. His basic training was at Lackland Air Force Base in San Antonio, Texas; he received overseas assignment in September of 1950. His overseas assignments included Hagaruri Air Base, Seoul Air Base and Kimpo Air Base. He returned to the United States in 1952 and completed his tour of duty in 1953 at Westover Field, Chicopee Falls, Massachusetts. He received his discharge on September 11, 1953. *Courtesy of Harry A. Ingram.*

Robert Boyce Harrill and Myrtice Hardin Harrill were married in 1966. Myrtice has been a Belk's buyer and a teacher's aide at Alexander School for sixteen years. Boyce worked for twenty years with U.S. General Accounting. The two went to the White House Lawn for President Ronald Reagan and Mrs. Nancy Reagan to present Boyce with the "Take Pride in America Award." Harrill had been the community, the county and the state winner; Governor Martin had presented him the state award. *Courtesy of Boyce and Myrtice Harrill.*

Airman Harry A. Ingram Jr. (in uniform), his mother (Meredith Ingram) and his younger brother (Jim Ingram) stand in front of their Church Street home in Cliffside in the summer of 1950, before Harry's deployment to Japan and Korea. *Courtesy of Jim Ingram.*

Jim Ingram remembers, as a high school student at Cliffside High School, "keeping up with the Korean War" with care. His older brother Harry was serving, and Jim followed his brother's service with interest and concern. Pictured above is tenth-grader Jim Ingram, younger brother of Harry A. Ingram Jr. Jim stands on the road between his home and the Boy Scout Field in Cliffside. *Courtesy of Jim Ingram.*

Jim Ingram would later enter the Marine Corps in September of 1957; he served as a platoon leader and was stationed at Quantico, Virginia, and Okinawa, Japan. Jim earned his B.S. in education from Western Carolina. *Courtesy of Jim Ingram.*

Another Cliffside resident entered service at about the same time as Jim. On September 9, 1950, after three years of college, Louise Hill enlisted. Louise had graduated from Cliffside High School, had completed nursing training at Spartanburg General Hospital (now Spartanburg Regional Medical Center) and had worked in the operating room of the old Mission Hospital in Asheville, North Carolina. *Courtesy of Louise Hill.*

Lieutenant Louise Hill's military assignments carried her to Fukuoka, Japan, where World War II American POWs had constructed many of the barracks. She served at Womack General Hospital, named for a Rutherford County Medal of Honor Recipient. Her life of service included Fort Sam Houston, the army hospital near Seoul and a nurses reserve unit at Oteen Veterans Hospital. *Courtesy of Louise Hill.*

Lieutenant Louise Hill's service took her to at least four more military hospitals before her discharge on January 1, 1966. Her medals included, among others, the National Defense Service Medal, the Korean Service Medal and the United Nations Service Medal. *Courtesy of Louise Hill.*

Staff Sergeant Fred Lee Hill enlisted in the United States Air Force on September 19, 1950, ten days after his sister Louise Hill joined. Fred served with the Sixty-seventh Recon Tech Squadron. While Fred served at Travis Air Force Base in California, Louise was in "the far, far East." Louise and Fred Lee Hill met in San Francisco and later in Fukuoka, Japan, where they enjoyed their reunion and their R and R. *Courtesy of Louise Hill.*

Before his enlistment, Fred Hill's last civilian job was as short order cook at Ron and Eddy's Restaurant in Forest City. For his military service Fred Lee Hill earned the Good Conduct Medal, the National Defense Service Medal, the Korean Service Medal and the United Nations Service Medal. *Courtesy of Louise Hill.*

Corporal Bobby Earl Franks performed his military duty with Headquarters Company, 3rd Battalion, 147th Infantry Regiment, at Fort Polk, Louisiana. *Courtesy of Shane Franks Atchley.*

Corporal Franks (second from left) stands in front of an M-4 Sherman tank while he attended the Armored School, Fort Knox, Kentucky. Franks trained as a tracked vehicle mechanic. Bobby Earl Franks died on June 29, 1969. *Courtesy of Shane Franks Atchley.*

Bostic native Robert Boyce Harrill enlisted in the U.S. Navy on January 31, 1951. Harrill, who was a Hospitalman, First Class, at the time of his discharge, served three years, eleven months and twelve days. Attached to both the Seabees and the U.S. Marines, Harrill served in Viegas, Puerto Rico; Newfoundland; Labrador; and Thule, Greenland. Life in Viegas, Puerto Rico, was quite primitive. Harrill learned to bathe, shave and brush his teeth with one helmet of water. *Courtesy of Robert Boyce Harrill.*

Robert Boyce Harrill served aboard the USS *Tanner* (AGS-15). In the icy waters (particularly around Thule, Greenland) the ship often had an icebreaker to go before it. Here is Harrill (left) at his duty post with Ray Foster of Tennessee. He remembers the dark hours in Greenland and the warnings to enlisted men that the natives could easily contract disease from the outsiders. They stand in front of a twin forty-millimeter Bofors gun mount. *Courtesy of Robert Boyce Harrill.*

In Greenland, one of the main modes of transportation and for fishing the waters was the canoe. This was a typical scene from the bluffs around the coast of Greenland. *Courtesy of Robert Boyce Harrill.*

Robert Boyce Harrill recalls that onboard the *Tanner* there was a stowaway: a dog! The crew named the visitor "Stow," short for Stowaway. The men hid the animal and passed it from hand to hand when inspections were imminent. For his services Robert Boyce Harrill earned, among others, the National Defense Service Medal and the Good Conduct Medal. *Courtesy of Robert Boyce Harrill.*

The CCF Spring Offensive and the UN Command Summer/Fall Offensive

APRIL 22, 1951–NOVEMBER 27, 1951

In retrospect, General Douglas MacArthur made at least two serious miscalculations. First, he failed to understand the concept of limited war. Second, he did not anticipate the reaction the Red Chinese would feel at having their borders threatened.

On March 20, 1951, MacArthur wrote a letter to House Minority Leader Joe Martin for publication. The contents publicly advocated using Chinese Nationalist Forces to invade Mainland China—a decided change in U.S. foreign policy. MacArthur's statement was in marked disobedience to President Truman's guidelines that military leaders not publicly criticize U.S. foreign policy. When the letter reached the press, President Truman viewed the letter as insubordination.

On April 11, 1951, President Truman relieved MacArthur of command. MacArthur was in Tokyo when he first learned of the change of command through a radio bulletin. Matthew B. Ridgway, who had been promoted to general, assumed full command of the Far Eastern and Korean commands.

During this time UN forces attacked CCF forces at a series of locations mainly remembered by their code names: Operation Rugged, Line Kansas, Line Utah, Line Wyoming, and Piledriver. These central Korean battles occurred in an area to be known as the Iron Triangle.

With the success of the UN attacks, the Soviet Union's UN representative announced that he believed the Korean War could be settled and that discussions should begin between the warring parties. The Soviet's delegate anticipated a cease-fire and armistice. The Chinese Communists signaled their agreement in a communiqué released from Beijing. President Truman authorized Ridgway to arrange armistice talks with the enemy. The talks began at the town of Kaesong, which was located in "no man's land"—between the front lines. During these talks, military action could continue. This first series of talks lasted approximately six weeks before the Communists ceased participation on August 22, 1951.

Operations accelerated with the discontinuation of negotiations. Three famous battles marked the violence in late September/early October. The battles were the Punch Bowl, Bloody Ridge and Heartbreak Ridge. These battles had ended successfully for UN forces by October 12, 1951. On October 25, 1951, negotiations restarted at Panmunjon village. Peace talks would continue through November 27 without a conclusion.

According to "Korean War Medal of Honor Recipients," the MOH citation for Jerry Crump reads:

> *The President of the United States in the name of The Congress takes pleasure in presenting the Medal of Honor to CRUMP, JERRY K.*
> *Rank and organization: Corporal, U.S. Army, Company L, 7th Infantry Regiment, 3rd Infantry Division.*
> *Place and date: Near Chorwon, Korea, 6 and 7 September 1951.*
> *Entered service at: Forest City, N.C. Born: 18 February 1933, Charlotte, N.C. G.O. No.: 68, 11 July 1951.*
> *Citation.*
> *Cpl. Crump, a member of Company L, distinguished himself by conspicuous gallantry and outstanding courage above and beyond the call of duty in action against the enemy. During the night a numerically superior hostile force launched an assault against his platoon on Hill 284, overrunning friendly positions and swarming into the sector. Cpl. Crump repeatedly exposed himself to deliver effective fire into the ranks of the assailants, inflicting numerous casualties. Observing 2 enemy soldiers endeavoring to capture a friendly machine gun, he charged and killed both with his bayonet, regaining control of the weapon. Returning to his position, now occupied by 4 of his wounded comrades, he continued his accurate fire into enemy troops surrounding his emplacement. When a hostile soldier hurled a grenade into the position, Cpl. Crump immediately flung himself over the missile, absorbing the blast with his body and saving his comrades from death or serious injury. His aggressive actions had so inspired his comrades that a spirited counterattack drove the enemy from the perimeter. Cpl. Crump's heroic devotion to duty, indomitable fighting spirit, and willingness to sacrifice himself to save his comrades reflect the highest credit upon himself, the infantry and the U.S. Army.*

Corporal Jerry Kirt Crump entered service at Forest City, North Carolina, on July 11, 1951. He earned the Medal of Honor during the Korean War. A street in Lincolnton bears the name of and honors Jerry Crump. *Courtesy of Korean Medal of Honor Recipients.*

Jerry Crump's twin brother Harry Crump served in the United States Army. He suffered the loss of an eye, a piece of shrapnel lodged in his sinus cavity, and the reconstruction of his face. Harry Crump rehabilitated for twenty-one months at a hospital in Pennsylvania. Harry Crump has lived in Lincolnton, North Carolina, for much of his life and has been active in the VFW Post 1706 since 1952. *Courtesy of Palmer and Frances Bailey.*

Private First Class Fonzer Maloy Yelton, a Rutherford County native, served as a cannoneer in Battery B, Eighty-second Field Artillery Battalion, First Cavalry Division. Yelton's artillery battery consisted of 155-millimeter howitzers and could pulverize their targets from a distance of up to ten miles. This trooper received the Good Conduct Medal, the Army of Occupation with Japan Clasp, the National Defense Service Medal, the Korean Service Medal with three Bronze Service Stars and the United Nations Service Medal. *Courtesy of Fonzer Maloy Yelton.*

Sergeant Donald Ray Peterson served split tours of duty. His assignments carried him from Keesler Air Force Base in Mississippi; to Shepperd Air Force Base in Texas; to Travis Air Force Base in California; to Pusan in Korea. During his Korean service, Peterson was a refrigeration and air conditioning specialist. His unit manufactured and dispensed hydrogen, nitrogen and oxygen used on Air Force aircraft. *Courtesy of Donald Ray Peterson.*

This 1952 Christmas celebration that Donald Ray Peterson has preserved on film depicts the interior of air personnel quarters. Peterson is the second from left. He recalled one night in particular when the North Koreans shelled his unit with artillery and mortar fire. *Courtesy of Donald Ray Peterson.*

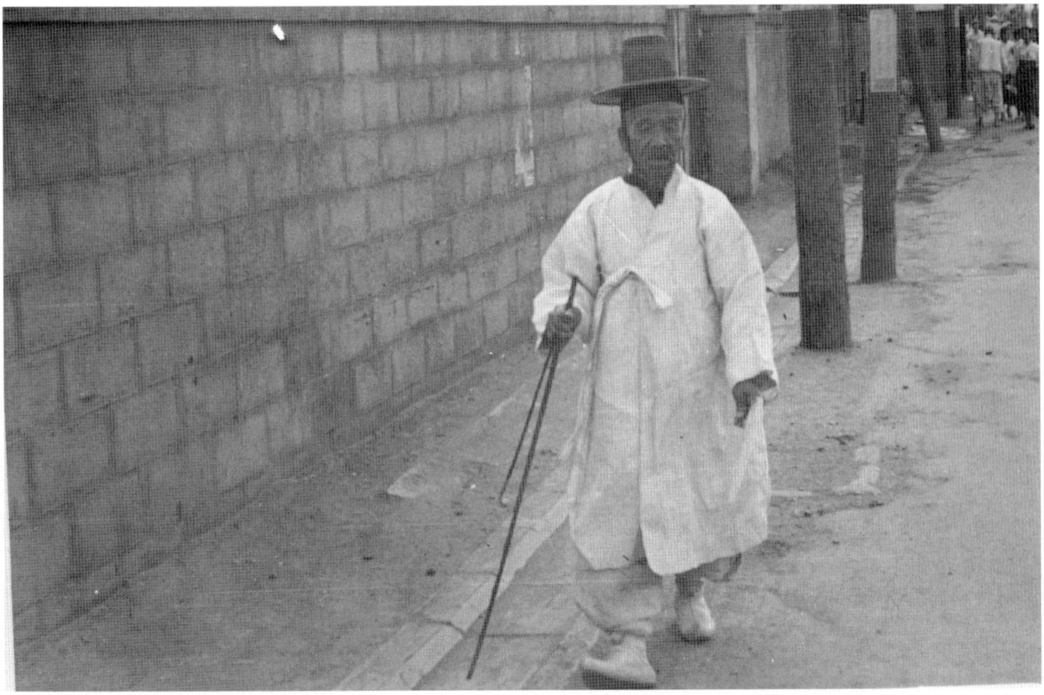

Sergeant Donald Ray Peterson made this photo of a native Korean. The man is wearing his native dress as he walks down the streets of Pusan. The horsehair hat was a part of the Korean costume. *Courtesy of Donald Ray Peterson.*

The children in Korea touched the heart of Sergeant Peterson. *Courtesy of Donald Ray Peterson.*

Sergeant Robert L. Bailey, Second Infantry Division, received training as a medical aidman at Japan Logistical Command Medical Service Technicians School. He entered service on March 5, 1951; on April 2, 1952, he wrote home that he was impressed with the helicopter rescue of the wounded, even on the front lines. *Courtesy of Keith M. Bailey.*

Robert L. Bailey participated in the Korean battles of Heartbreak and Bloody Ridges. Bailey often patrolled the snow-blanketed Korean hills. The men's tents are evident in the background. On April 2, 1952, the son of Mr. and Mrs. H.C. Bailey wrote that he was OK and had seen the artillery flashing. He mentioned the birthday cake he had received from home for his twenty-second birthday on March 24. *Courtesy of Keith M. Bailey.*

Spindale native Boyce Elmer Ware served in the Medical Company, 4th Battalion, 180th Infantry Regiment, 45th Infantry Division ("Thunderbirds") from October 1951 to August 1953. Private First Class Ware participated at the Battle of Heartbreak Ridge. For his services Ware received (among others) the Korean Service Medal with two Bronze Service Stars and the United Nations Service Medal: Overseas Bar. *Courtesy of Boyce E. Ware.*

Senior Master Sergeant William Stanford Jackson received the Korean Service Medal, the Air Force Outstanding Unit Award, the Air Force Longevity Service Award with four Oak Leaf Clusters, the Air Force Medal and the Air Force Good Conduct Medal (AFGCM). Jackson stands before the soldiers' welcomed Korean lodging place: a tent—decidedly better than the ground. *Courtesy of William Stanford Jackson.*

When Forest City native Thomas Eugene Morrow received his draft notice from Local Board 82, he was an employee at Stonecutter Mills; he entered service on November 29, 1950. Morrow was posted to Headquarters and Headquarters Battery, 198th Field Artillery Battalion, 31st Infantry Regiment, 7th Infantry Division ("Bayonet") after his basic training. This photograph shows the mountainous terrain that makes up the central portion of the Korean Peninsula. *Courtesy of Thomas Eugene Morrow.*

This photograph shows the living quarters of men in the field artillery. The authors are sure that "camping out" soon lost its charm. For his services Sergeant Morrow would earn the Combat Infantryman's Badge, the Korean Service Medal with Bronze Service Star and the United Nations Service Medal. His unit received the Meritorious Unit Citation. *Courtesy of Thomas Eugene Morrow.*

William Stanford Jackson retired from the United States Air Force on July 1, 1971, as a senior master sergeant. During his time in Korea, he served in A Company, 839th Engineers, who constructed Air Base Number K-55 near Osan, Korea. This location thirty miles south of Seoul served as a base for heavy bombers. Jackson described his time in Korea as "uneventful." *Courtesy of William Stanford Jackson.*

Sergeant Robert L. Bailey kneels in the middle of his "Main Street." For his services, Sergeant Robert L. Bailey received the Combat Medical Badge, Korean Service Medal with two Bronze Service Stars and the United Nations Service Medal. His letter home indicated that he had been "put in" for the Silver and Bronze Medals. *Courtesy of Keith M. Bailey.*

The Second Korean Winter

NOVEMBER 28, 1951–APRIL 1952

Despite the earlier peace talks, no settlement of hostilities had been reached by November of 1951. Angry confrontations regarding prisoners of war, repatriation and prisoner exchange had prompted a volatile situation at UN Command Prison Camp I on Koje-Do Island. The prisoners of war captured the U.S. camp commander and demanded an admission of inhumane treatment of prisoners; the inmates declared that the cruelties had caused many to decline repatriation to the North. The new camp commander, to obtain his predecessor's release, signed a statement admitting to instances of bloodshed and slayings of POWs.

During the troubles at Koje-Do, General Ridgway received transfer to NATO command in Europe. General Mark W. Clark assumed the command of the Far East upon Ridgway's new duty.

General Clark immediately repudiated the Koje-Do camp commander's damaging "admissions." He assigned Brigadier General Haydon L. Boatner to rectify the POW situation by assigning the POW to smaller compounds.

Bitter hostilities continued on the front. These costly battles resulted in many casualties, but the lines remained virtually unchanged by spring of 1952.

Corporal Hazel Baker Yount was born April 4, 1927, in the Duncan's Creek Township. He was one of seven children of Noah Hartsell Yount and Minnie Jane Toney Yount. Yount farmed until he entered service. Yount married Christine Norville and they had two daughters, Wanda Kay and Hazel Denise. His wife indicated he talked very little about his service although his mail did go to the Army Chemical Center in Edgewood, Maryland. Yount died on February 5, 1983.

According to "Korean Medal of Honor Recipients," Private First Class Bryant Womack's citation of March 12, 1952, reads:

> *The President of the United States in the name of The Congress takes pleasure in presenting the Medal of Honor to BRYANT WOMACK.*

Rank and organization: Private First Class, U.S. Army, Medical Company, 14th Infantry Regiment, 25th Infantry Division.
Place and date: Near Sokso-ri, Korea, 12 March 1952. Entered service at: Mill Springs, N.C. Birth: Mill Springs, N.C. G.O. No.: 5, 12 January 1953.
Citation:
Pfc. Womack distinguished himself by conspicuous gallantry above and beyond the call of duty in action against the enemy. Pfc. Womack was the only medical aid man attached to a night combat patrol when sudden contact with a numerically superior enemy produced numerous casualties. Pfc. Womack went immediately to their aid, although this necessitated exposing himself to a devastating hail of enemy fire, during which he was seriously wounded. Refusing medical aid for himself, he continued moving among his comrades to administer aid. While he was aiding 1 man, he was again struck by enemy mortar fire, this time suffering the loss of his right arm. Although he knew the consequences should immediate aid not be administered, he still refused aid and insisted that all efforts be made for the benefit of others that were wounded. Although unable to perform the task himself, he remained on the scene and directed others in first aid techniques. The last man to withdraw, he walked until he collapsed from loss of blood, and died a few minutes later while being carried by his comrades. The extraordinary heroism, outstanding courage, and unswerving devotion to his duties displayed by Pfc. Womack reflect the utmost distinction upon himself and uphold the esteemed traditions of the U.S. Army.

Private First Class Bryant Womack, U.S. Army, Medical Company, Fourteenth Infantry Regiment, Twenty-fifth Infantry Division, was the Ninety-seventh Medal of Honor (MOH) Recipient and one of fourteen "Tropical Lightning" soldiers to receive the MOH. Rutherford County claims this hero who has a hospital named in his honor at Fort Bragg, North Carolina. *Courtesy of "Korean Medal of Honor Recipients."*

Corporal Hazel Baker Yount served with the 9710th TSU (ACC MD), DET 1, a confidential unit. Yount's discharge paper has much of its information redacted. During his tour, Yount was stationed in Maryland, Mississippi, Idaho, Georgia and Florida. For his services he received the Good Conduct Medal and the National Defense Service Medal. *Courtesy of Christine N. Yount and daughters.*

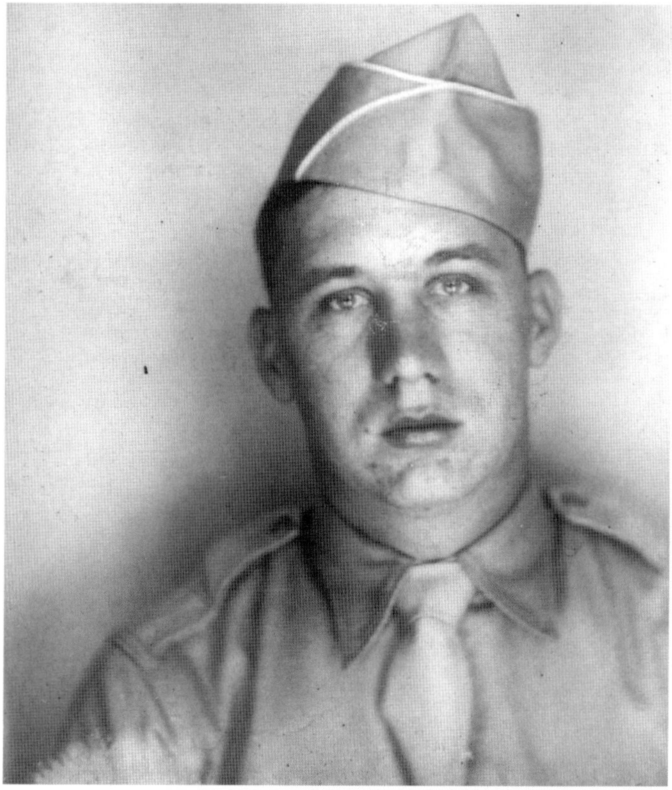

Sergeant Norman Turner Deese served in Battery SV, Seventy-third Armored Field Artillery Battalion. For his services in Korea, Sergeant Deese received the National Defense Service Medal, the Korean Service Medal with three Bronze Service Stars and the United Nations Service Medal. Deese remembers that the mess hall food was good and that they received Lucky Strike cigarettes. *Courtesy of Norman Turner Deese.*

Corporal Norman Turner Deese has retained for about half a century this photograph of Seoul, Korea. It reminds him of an earlier time and place in his life. *Courtesy of Norman Turner Deese.*

Corporal Norman Turner Deese's SV Battery prepared artillery positions near the front lines. *Courtesy of Norman Turner Deese.*

Yeoman Third Class William Horace White Jr. entered the U.S. Navy on May 23, 1951. He served aboard the USS *Wisconsin* (BB-64), USS *Forrestal* (CVA-59) and the USS *English* (DD-696). He worked with a sixteen-inch gun crew in the projectile magazine on the *Wisconsin*. While aboard *Forrestal*, White had duty with Fleet Aircraft Service Squadron 121 at Chincoteague, Virginia. White earned the Korean Service Medal with Bronze Service Star, the National Defense Service Medal, the United Nations Service Medal and the Korean Presidential Unit Citation. *Courtesy of Tim D. White.*

Ellenboro native Bobby Joe Kendrick and his wife Betty Sue Barnette Kendrick share their wedding day. Kendrick earned the Good Conduct Medal, the Korean Service Medal with one Silver and one Bronze Service Star, the United Nations Service Medal, the National Defense Service Medal, the China Service Medal, the Republic of Korea Presidential Unit Citation and the Navy Occupation Medal (Japan). *Courtesy of Betty Sue Barnette Kendrick.*

Walker Benton McCrary, Machine Repairman/Fireman 1/C, served in the United States Navy from 1950–54. Walker Benton McCrary's duty was on board the USS *Antietam,* an Essex class aircraft carrier. *Courtesy of W.B. McCrary.*

MRFN 1/C McCrary was one of 3,500 men aboard *Antietam,* an Essex class aircraft carrier; this photo shows his station. *Antietam* made four cruises off Korea with Task Force 77 between November 1951 and March 1952; her air group flew over 6,000 sorties, which included combat air patrol, logistics interdictions, reconnaissance patrols, anti-submarine patrols and night-heckler missions. *Courtesy of W.B. McCrary.*

W.B. McCrary received this photograph from his commander. The inscription reads: To you for the part you played in making a fighting ship a winning ship. The circle is over McCrary's face. *Courtesy of W.B. McCrary.*

This photograph of Corporal Norman Turner Deese reflects the barren countryside that was very much a part of his daily life when he was stationed overseas. *Courtesy of Norman Turner Deese.*

Verner Hardin with the Sixty-Third Troop Carrier Wing (Heavy). He served in Japan as a teletype operator in a Communications Squadron for about 2 ½ years (from December 1951 until May of 1954). When Hardin ended his tour of duty in July of 1955, he had attained the rank of staff sergeant. He earned the Good Conduct Medal, the National Defense Service Medal, the Korean Service Medal, and the United Nations Korean Service Medal. His unit received the Outstanding Unit Award. *Courtesy of Verner Hardin.*

The Summer and Fall of 1952

MAY–NOVEMBER 1952

The enemy became increasingly bold in the spring of 1952. The UN troops met the hostilities with resistance. The Forty-fifth Infantry Division alone suffered more than one thousand casualties during the month of June.

During the first part of 1952, the UN forces waged a war of containment. Small-scale attacks continued through July. Torrential August rains prohibited much activity on both sides, but September brought increased artillery and mortar fire from CCF forces to support renewed attacks upon UN command forces.

The summer of 1952 saw a marked increase in the air war. UN aircraft struck at enemy supply centers, troop concentrations, power plants, factories, road and rail networks. This air support was valuable to frontline troops; the use of napalm could burn out bunkers, trenches, gun placements and lines of communication. On August 29, 1952, the U.S. Air Force carried out the heaviest raid of the Korean War on Pyongyang, the North Korean capital.

In October 1952 enemy attacks produced some of the most intense fighting in more than a year. The ten-day battles around two map locations (Hill 281 and Hill 395) resulted in a body count of over two thousand CCF troops.

While stationed at Yongdung Po, Cliffside native "Ed" Wright Scruggs, on his day off, visited boyhood friend Private First Class A.C. Greene. A.C. was in another unit stationed nearby, and Ed discovered that it was A.C.'s birthday (July 19). They spent the entire day talking, swapping stories and relaxing. A.C., who had grown up on River Street in Cliffside, was serving in the Seventy-sixth Engineer Construction Battalion. Ed returned to Greene's tent about two weeks later, looking forward to another visit with his friend. He was devastated to find that A.C. had been killed in action.

The 514th/54th WX Reconnaissance Squadron to which Chief Master Sergeant Darrell Franklin Skinner was assigned had other interesting duties, like locating and tracking typhoons;

Serving with the U.S. Air Force on Okinawa was Claude Nelon with the 307th Bomb Wing. Major Nelon flew missions in a B-29 Super Fortress bomber to interdict the North Koreans/CCF forces on the Korean Peninsula. In this immediate postwar photo, Brigadier General Carmichael commends Major Nelon and his crew upon their selection as combat crew for November 1953. Nelon dedicated this image to his wife Helen. At his 1974 retirement Command Pilot Nelon had flown ten thousand hours. *Courtesy of Claude R. Nelon.*

they were able to penetrate eighteen separate typhoons. The squadron also performed search and rescue missions. During his career Skinner served on every continent except Antarctica; he even served on Air Force One at the time of the presidency of George Herbert Walker Bush. During his travels Skinner saw such world leaders as Chinese Premier Mao Tse-tung and Israeli Prime Minister Golda Meir.

Darrell Franklin Skinner retired on September 30, 1977. He earned, among others, the following medals: the Good Conduct Medal with three Oak Leaf Clusters, the Korean Service Medal, the United Nations Service Medal, the National Defense Service Medal with Bronze Service Star, the Vietnam Commendation Medal, the Air Medal with four Oak Leaf Clusters, the Air Force Longevity Medal with three Oak Leaf Clusters, the Air Force Commendation Medal with two Oak Leaf Clusters and the Presidential Service Badge.

Darrell Skinner had a second career: he worked for the Department of State from 1979 to 1990. He served in Africa for eight years and in Europe for three years. From 1990 to 1999 he served part-time to the U.S. Department of State Africa; he reached the rank of GS-11. He returned to Rutherford County in 2000.

Although Bill David Ingram's stay in North Korea came near the close of the war, the *Wantuck* earned four battle stars. The Marines were pulling back south of the thirty-eighth parallel, and the *Wantuck* performed some gunfire support in the hills above Wonson Harbor and transported some special teams to Pusan. He recalled "visiting Inchon Harbor after General MacArthur had pulled off a successful attack on the North Koreans and driven them back." Ingram retired on May 25, 1971, with the rank of chief radioman. His poem "The Dreamer—1945" embellishes an early page of this book.

Colonel Nelon served in the U.S. Air Force for thirty-one years and nine months. He was aerospace professor at Syracuse University, commander of the Air Force ROTC and director of the Russian Language Program for Military Personnel, Syracuse University. He earned the Good Conduct Medal, the World War II Occupation Medal (Germany), the National Defense Service Medal, the Korean Service Medal, the United Nations Korean Service Medal and the Air Force Commendation Medal. *Courtesy of Claude R. Nelon.*

Private First Class James Mack Prescott enlisted in the United States Marine Corps in August of 1951. He served in the Anti-Tank Platoon of the Seventh Infantry Regiment of the First Marine Division. Prescott described his tour of duty as seeming "like a dream." *Courtesy of James Mack Prescott.*

When James Mack Prescott entered service, he stood 5 feet 7 inches tall and weighed 125 pounds. Prescott was only nineteen years of age. Home on furlough, James Mack Prescott visited his parents, Mr. and Mrs. McKinley Prescott, who were related to W.J. York, a former Rutherford County commissioner. Here he stands in front of their sparkling clean 1950 Chevrolet truck. *Courtesy of James Mack Prescott.*

James Mack Prescott recalled the cold of a Korean winter, the heat of a Korean summer and the night fighting on the peninsula. Here a young Prescott relaxes for a few moments as he waits for his laundry to dry and for his orders to return to the front line. Prescott recalled with pride his ability to use both an 81-millimeter mortar and a .50-caliber heavy machine gun. He admitted matter-of-factly that he could "put a bazooka round in your back pocket." *Courtesy of James Mack Prescott.*

Private First Class James Mack Prescott (right) receives the Purple Heart Medal for shrapnel wounds from a grenade or a mortar round that he received in action against Chinese Communist forces. His commanding officer, Lieutenant Colonel Anthony Caputo, presents the award at the Korean front. *Courtesy of James Mack Prescott.*

Corporal Willard Narce Bailey entered service March 5, 1951. He received assignment to the 462nd Quartermaster Laundry Company. *Courtesy of Gaynell Owens Bailey.*

Corporal Willard Narce Bailey was stationed at Baumholder, Germany. He earned the rank of corporal before his discharge. One of his duties was guarding the Berlin Wall. Among his medals was the Good Conduct Medal. *Courtesy of Gaynell Owens Bailey.*

On May 30, 1952, Willard Narce Bailey and Gaynell Owens Bailey were married in Gaffney, South Carolina, by the Honorable Probate Judge W.R. Douglas. The couple spent their honeymoon in the Lake Lure area; the photograph is from this happy time. *Courtesy of Gaynell Owens Bailey.*

Spindale resident Bill Osborne Howard enlisted in the United States Navy on February 2, 1952. He completed his boot camp at San Diego, California. *Courtesy of Bill Osborne Howard.*

Bill Osborne Howard's wife, Ann Blanton Howard, soon joined him in California. Bill and Ann were able to live in a "beautiful but small house on the beach in San Diego." *Courtesy of Ann Blanton Howard and Bill Osborne Howard.*

This picture shows (left to right) Ann Blanton Howard, Bill Howard, Bill's mother Ollie Miller Howard and Bill's father Ray Henry Howard (who celebrated his one hundredth birthday in November of 2005). Ray Henry Howard has long been a member of the Spindale Baptist Church. *Courtesy of Bill Osborne Howard.*

Hospitalman Second Class Bill Osborne Howard served aboard the USS *Magoffin* (APA-199), a type VC2-S-API. The *Magoffin* had a crew of about 536 men and displaced about 6,873 tons. Pictured here are crewmen of the USS *Magoffin*. *Courtesy of Bill Osborne Howard.*

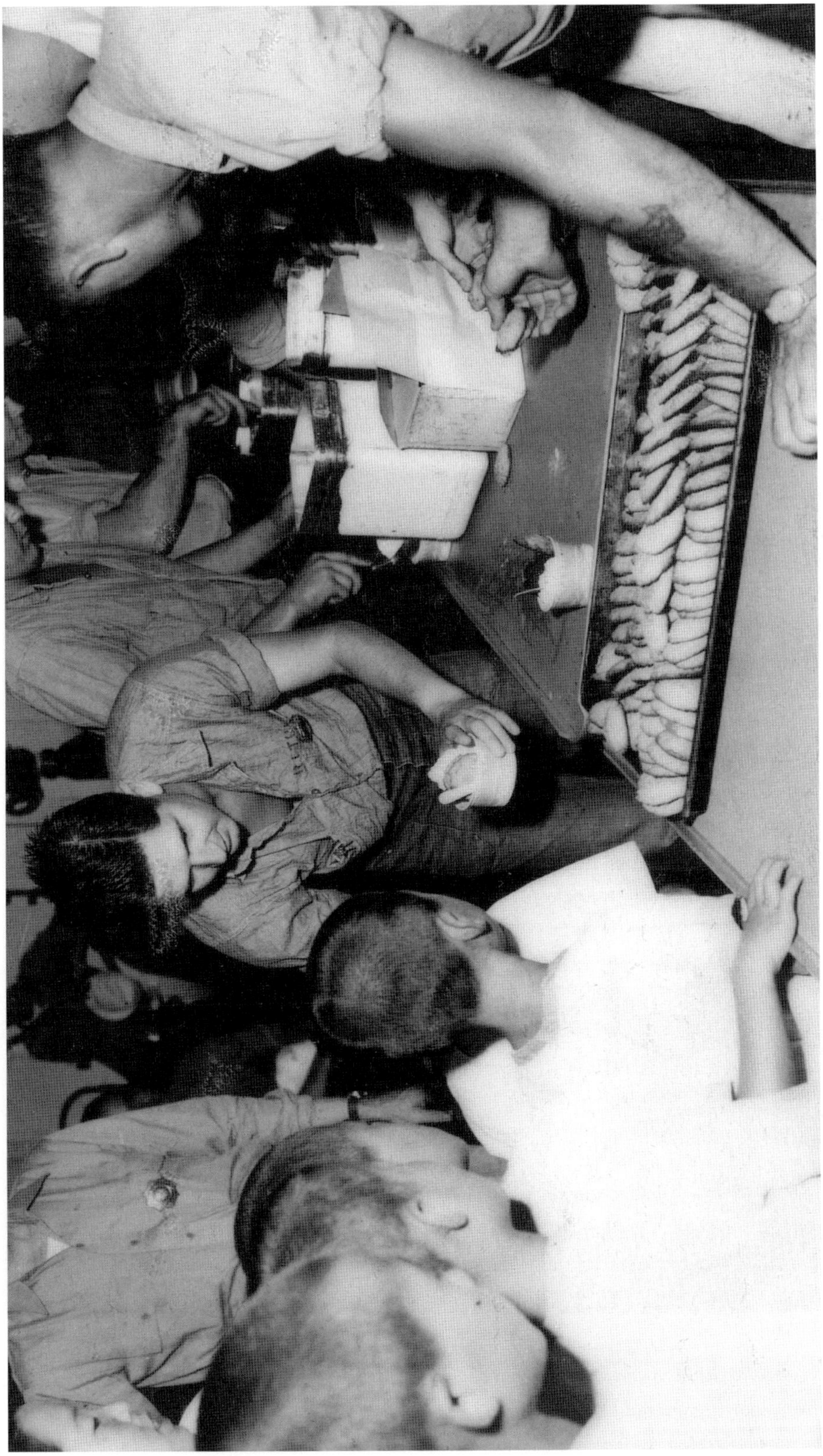

Here Bill Osborne Howard serves some sweets to orphan children visiting on board the USS *Magoffin* during Christmas. HM/2C Howard recalled visiting the Post Exchange (PX) in Seoul in 1952. A GI there told him, "The war must be over because the navy is in town." Howard has remembered, with good humor, this remark for more than half a century. After Korea, Howard received additional training at the United States Hospital Corps School at Portsmouth, Virginia. *Courtesy of Bill Osborne Howard.*

During the winter of 1952 while at Inchon Harbor, the crew of the USS *Magoffin* invited a group of Korean orphans to celebrate Christmas on board the ship. Here the captain and executive officer welcome the children. *Courtesy of Bill Osborne Howard.*

This Inchon Harbor sign greets the UN supply ships and crews and gives credit to the Twenty-first Transportation Medium Port that erected it. Howard finished his tour at the U.S. Naval Hospital in Jacksonville, Florida. He earned the Good Conduct Medal, the National Defense Service Medal, the Korean Service Medal with Bronze Service Star and the United Nations Service Medal. *Courtesy of Bill Osborne Howard.*

Cliffside native Ed Wright Scruggs served with the 741st Aircraft Control and Warning Squadron. He was in Colorado from September until November of 1950, when he was re-assigned to the K-16 Air Base at Yongdungpo on the Han River; he served with the 61st Aircraft Control and Warning Squadron, attached to the 1st Marine Division. *Courtesy of Ed Wright Scruggs.*

This photo shows A.C. Greene as a child in Mrs. John Tinkler's fifth-grade class at Cliffside School. A.C. is the tall boy who is standing beside Mrs. Tinkler in the back row. Judson "Bud" Crow Sr. recalls that A.C. was a quiet boy with a cross-handed grip when he played baseball. *Courtesy of Geraldine Wall and Judson Crow Sr.*

Airman First Class Ed W. Scruggs visited on board the hospital ship USS *Hope* and met his first cousin Lionel Scruggs, petty officer first class, U.S. Navy, on the launching pad. In Pusan, Scruggs met Cliffside friend Henry Campbell. Scruggs received his discharge from the USAF at Lackland Air Force Base on July 11, 1954. He earned the Good Conduct Medal, Korean Service Medal, the United Nations Korean Service Medal with Bronze Service Star and the National Defense Service Medal. *Courtesy of Ed Wright Scruggs.*

Ed. W. Scruggs expressed to the authors his pleasure and pride at being able to return to the fiftieth anniversary celebrations in Seoul, Korea, as a guest of the Korean government. Scruggs was touched to see on the Korean War Memorial in Seoul his friends' names, Vernon D. Stallings and A.C. Greene. One of the mementos that Ed Wright Scruggs brought home from the visit was a section of wire from the demilitarized zone (DMZ). *Courtesy of Ed Wright Scruggs.*

Rutherford County native Judson "Bud" Oren Crow Sr. was a friend of Ed W. Scruggs. Crow served in the USAF from December 3, 1950, until September 4, 1954. He performed the duties of a radio mechanic. *Courtesy of Judson "Bud" Oren Crow Sr.*

Judson "Bud" Oren Crow Sr. spent the Christmas of 1952 in the cork forest near Rabat-Sale, French Morocco. Bud (left) appears with fellow airman Andy Anderson and their Christmas tree. *Courtesy of Judson "Bud" Oren Crow Sr.*

By the Thanksgiving of 1953 Crow was serving "under the Ice Cap near the North Pole." He said the menu was very similar to that of the previous year. Crow received his discharge on September 3, 1954. He had attained the rank of staff sergeant and had earned the Good Conduct Medal and the National Defense Service Medal. *Courtesy of Judson "Bud" Oren Crow Sr.*

Chief Master Sergeant Darrell Franklin Skinner served in the United States Air Force from 1950 until his retirement in 1977. He received assignment to the 514th/54th WX Reconnaissance Squadron, based at Andersen Air Force Base on Guam and performed the duties of a flight radio operator. The purpose of the 54th Weather Reconnaissance Squadron was to provide weather information and forecasts to the bomber squadrons supporting the operations of the United Nations in Korea. *Courtesy of Darrell Franklin Skinner.*

Also serving during the Korean War was Darrell Franklin Skinner's brother, Bobby Lee Skinner. Whereas Darrell Franklin Skinner served with the United States Air Force, however, Bobby Lee Skinner served in the United States Navy from 1951 to 1954. Bobby, a Marine oiler, served on USS *Wisconsin*, which ported at Guam. Darrell was able to visit him aboard the ship and received a tour of the ship. Bobby served three years and nine months in the navy. *Courtesy of Margaret Skinner Green, Darrell Skinner and Brenda J. Smith (oldest daughter).*

Both Darrell Franklin Skinner and Bobby Lee Skinner were brothers of Margaret Skinner Green and the children of Lila Cole and William Lee Skinner. Margaret is familiar with the military because, in addition to her two brothers, her husband Dwight Green and his brother Edgar Green had served in World War II. Bobby earned the Korean Service Medal, the United Nations Service Medal, Good Conduct Medal (twice) and the Presidential Unit Citation. *Courtesy of Margaret Skinner Green, Darrell Skinner and family.*

Entering service on August 2, 1947, was Ted H. Newton. This county native served in the United States Army and earned the rank of second lieutenant. During the Korean War he served in counter-intelligence with the Third Infantry Division. For his services he received the Good Conduct Medal, the National Defense Service Medal, the Korean Service Medal with two Bronze Service Stars and the United Nations Service Medal. *Courtesy of Ted H. Newton.*

Private First Class Harry Claude Scruggs of Cliffside served as a medic. Harry had worked summers at Broughton State Hospital; he received orders to serve as ward technician in the mental ward at the Osaka Army Hospital 8009th AU. "I was the luckiest medic in the Korean War because I saw Korea only across the Straits of Japan." After serving overseas one year, three months and four days, Scruggs received the Korean Service and UN Service Medal upon his 1953 discharge. *Courtesy of Eric C. Scruggs.*

Bill David Ingram served with the North Carolina National Guard, Battery B, 112th FA BN, from 1950 until 1952. He attained the rank of corporal and served as company clerk. His discharge from the NCNG came on January 3, 1952; he enlisted in the U.S. Navy the next day. Ingram served aboard the USS *Wantuck* (APD-125). He participated in amphibious operations near Wonsan, North Korea; Siriko, Korea; Inchon Harbor, South Korea; and Pusan, South Korea. *Courtesy of Bill David Ingram.*

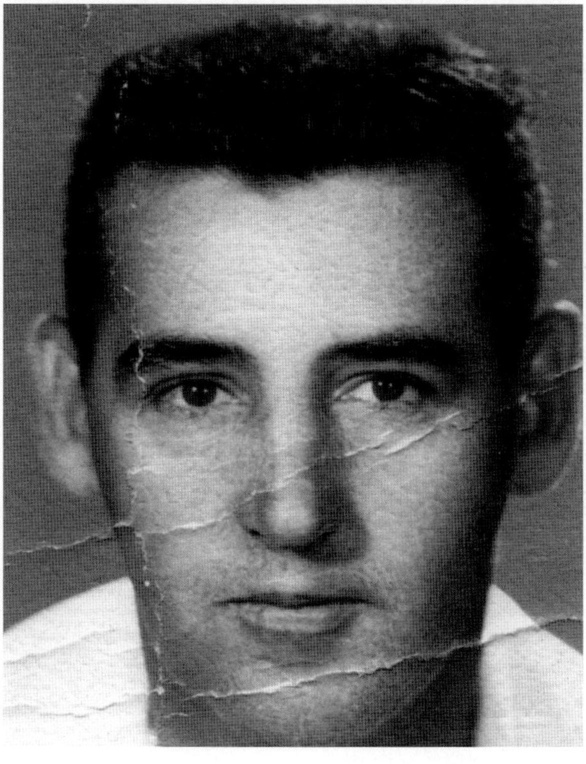

Master Sergeant Roy Elmer Harris, Cliffside native and signal intelligence operations chief, served twice in Korea. The twelfth child of C.C. Harris and Bertha Jones Harris, this twenty-year veteran retired in 1965 from Headquarters and Headquarters Company, USASATR, Fort Devens, Massachusetts. Harris, an expert with the M-1 carbine, earned the Good Conduct Medal (four times), National Defense Service Medal, the World War II Victory Medal, Armed Forces Expeditionary Medal and Army of Occupation (Germany). *Courtesy of Patricia C. Harris.*

Daniel Leroy Briscoe was another Rutherford County native who served his country during the Korean War. Daniel Briscoe (left) is here pictured with a friend, Ernest Crook. *Courtesy of the Briscoe and Crook families.*

Brothers Charles (oldest), Billy and Jimmy Gibson all served in the Air Force. Jimmy Gibson proudly reported that they were the only three brothers to serve as Air Force pilots on active duty in the history of the U.S. Air Force. Charles and Billy were World War II fighter pilots. Charles (now deceased) served in China in the Fourteenth Air Force; he retired as a lieutenant after serving twenty-six years. Billy served in Europe in the Eighth Air Force. Jimmy was a military air transport service pilot during the Korean War. Here Jimmy appears with headphones as an aviation cadet in San Angelo, Texas. *Courtesy of Jimmy Gibson.*

Jimmy enters his AT-6 trainer in the accompanying photo. Jimmy served four and a half years as a MATS captain and aircraft commander. Jimmy returned to Forest City after his discharge. He has served fourteen years on the town council and in 2006 is in his second term as Forest City Mayor. *Courtesy of Jimmy Gibson.*

Here Billy Gibson (right) stands with brother Jimmy Gibson (left) in front of a C-119 at Reese Air Base in Lubbock, Texas. Billy served thirty-one years and retired as a colonel. He now makes his home in McLean, Virginia. Billy served in the Pentagon for eighteen years. *Courtesy of Jimmy Gibson.*

Staff Sergeant Joe W. Goings served with the 330th Ordnance Company (Field Supply), 3rd Battalion, 180th Infantry Regiment, 45th Infantry Division. For his services in Korea he earned the Combat Infantryman's Badge, the Korean Service Medal with Bronze Service Star, United Nation Service Medal, National Defense Service Medal, Army Occupation Service Medal (Japan) and the Good Conduct Medal. *Courtesy of Joe W. Goings.*

Private Jonah Cochran served as an Infantryman, Company H, Twenty-sixth Infantry Regiment, First Infantry Division. Private Cochran was stationed in Germany. *Courtesy of Jonah Cochran.*

Jonah Cochran was in service from January of 1949 to February of 1953; he had signed up for three years, but the military extended his term by nine months. Jonah served overseas for two years and nine months. He received the Occupation Medal (Germany). This photograph shows a view of the Germany that he knew well. *Courtesy of Jonah Cochran.*

Jonah Cochran's photograph shows some of the devastation from war. This image shows the material damage that often accompanies the damage to life in wartime. *Courtesy of Jonah Cochran.*

Here Jonah Cochran and comrades are photographed with their Jeep armed with a Browning, .30-caliber machine gun, water-cooled. *Courtesy of Jonah Cochran.*

Technical Sergeant Robert Bruce Quick served in the military a total of twenty-three years. While in Korea, he had duty with the 762nd AC&W Squadron (Air Defense Command). Sergeant Quick expressed to the authors the pleasure he received in training his German Shepard. *Courtesy of Robert Bruce Quick.*

This photo shows the Eighth Air Police, Canine Section that Robert Quick worked with on a regular basis. *Courtesy of Robert Bruce Quick.*

George W. Jones of Ellenboro enlisted in the United States Navy on October 24, 1951. He trained at the San Diego Naval Training Center and served aboard both USS *Iowa* (BB-61) in a sixteen-inch gun turret and the heavy cruiser USS *Salem* (CA-139). Aboard *Iowa,* Jones was in active combat off the Korean coast. *Salem* ("pride of the Sixth Fleet") never fired its guns in anger. George was overseas three years, six months and twenty-one days. He earned the National Defense Service Medal, Navy Occupation Medal (Japan), United Nations Service Medal and Korean Service Medal (Bronze Service Star). *Courtesy of George W. Jones.*

Gunner's Mate Third Burton Jay Lyles entered the U.S. Navy in September 1950. He was fire control director to the USS *Los Angeles* (CA-135), the first naval vessel to take enemy fire; it "was struck twice by North Korean counter-battery fire and suffered casualties." With its eight-inch guns to pound enemy positions, it conducted fire support and interdiction missions from Hungnam on the east coast to Haeju on the west coast to support UN Command Forces. Lyles earned the National Defense Service Medal, Korean Service Medal, United Nations Service Medal and Good Conduct Medal. *Courtesy of Burton Jay Lyles.*

Jefferson Bostic Earley Sr. enlisted in the United States Army on December 15, 1950. With fellow members of the Supply-4 Section of the 773rd Tank Battalion, Earley (third from left, back row) stands near a sign at Fort Benning, Georgia. Earley received special training in automotive maintenance at Fort Jackson, South Carolina, and in track vehicle mechanics at the Armored School, Fort Knox, Kentucky. Earley received assignment to Headquarters and Service Company, 773rd Tank Battalion (Heavy), which earned the Meritorious Unit Citation. *Courtesy of Jefferson Bailey Earley Sr.*

The son of Mary Alice Smith Earley and David Russell Earley Sr., the 1947 Tri-High School graduate Jefferson Bostic Earley Sr. performed his entire tour of duty in the United States. He received his discharge on December 14, 1952, and resumed his civilian career with McDaniel-Smith Pontiac in Forest City, North Carolina. Earley retired in 1994 after many years of employment in the new car industry from Beam Chevrolet, where he had been business manager. *Courtesy of Jefferson Bailey Earley Sr.*

Technical Sergeant J.D. Beaver, command post controller, Headquarters Squadron, Seventieth Bombardment Wing, served from 1949 to 1967 and earned the Good Conduct Medal, the Korean Service Medal, the National Defense Service Medal and the United Nations Service Medal after "devoted and dedicated service." His citation from Colonel William R. Brown, Headquarters Squadron, Seventieth Bombardment Wing (SAC), Clinton-Sherman Air Force Base, Oklahoma, said he warranted "the gratitude of the American people." Technical Sergeant Beaver served in Okinawa and Japan. *Courtesy of Opal Beaver.*

Donald Jones Carpenter enlisted in the United States Navy on July 21, 1948. He served aboard the LST 898, where he was an electrician's mate second class. Carpenter was stationed in Adak, Alaska, where he ran the movie projector for the Helmet Creek Theater. He has kept two tickets as a souvenir for a half century. *Courtesy of Donald Jones Carpenter.*

With the outbreak of hostilities on the Korean Peninsula, Carpenter, an electrician's mate, received assignment to the hospital ship *Repose*. As a crewman, Carpenter helped to take the ship into Chinnampo, the port city of Pyongyang. The eight hundred-patient ship was the largest ship to have entered that port up until that time. The son of Mr. and Mrs. Hoyle B. Carpenter of Forest City, he completed his tour of duty upon the USS LST 898. He earned the Good Conduct Medal, the Korean Service Medal, the United Nations Service Medal and the Navy Occupation (Japan). *Courtesy of Donald Jones Carpenter.*

Quick's fondest memory was saluting the flag and returning home. Technical Sergeant Quick received for his services the Good Conduct Medal, the Korean Service Medal, the National Defense Service Medal and the United Nations Service Medal. *Courtesy of Robert Bruce Quick.*

Julian Edward Padgett served with the 512th Signal Base Maintenance Company as a cable splicer after a five-month course in splicing cable. Private First Class Padgett served in Germany for three years, three months and twenty-seven days. He received the National Defense Service Medal and the Occupation Medal (Germany). He entered service in May of 1952 and received his discharge on April 19, 1954. *Courtesy of Frances Padgett.*

The Third Korean Winter

DECEMBER 1, 1952–APRIL 30, 1953

Armistice talks continued. A main obstacle to the settlement of hostilities had been the subject of POWs and their repatriation.

November of 1952 brought a presidential election to the United States. After twenty years of Democratic leadership, the country chose World War II military hero General of the Army Dwight D. Eisenhower as president. Eisenhower in his campaign had pledged to go to Korea to implement a plan for quickly settling the Korean conflict. After his inauguration in January of 1953, Eisenhower forcefully informed the North Koreans, Russians and the Chinese that the United States would move decisively and would use all our weapons without hesitation.

General Mark Clark in February 1953 proposed an exchange of sick and wounded prisoners. There was no response in the deadlock at Panmunjon. The break in the negotiations finally came about three weeks after the death of Soviet dictator Joseph Stalin on March 5, 1953. The enemy delegates to the peace talks now responded favorably to Clark's proposal of prisoner exchange for those who were ill or wounded.

While home on furlough in 1952, Mike Flack received his assignment to the 9330th TSU Ordnance Unit at the Redstone Arsenal in Huntsville, Alabama, where he was able to work directly with Wehrner von Braun, the rocket scientist. Flack drove von Braun and other scientists to White Sands Proving Ground in New Mexico, helped fuel the first Redstone rocket, and participated in its launch. Mike said, "I helped fire the first Redstone rocket…I would not swap my military experience for a college degree…My military career has been the most interesting part of my life." Mike Flack retired from the Armed Forces of the United States on February 3, 1961, with the rank of sergeant.

Mike Flack, of the Union Mills area, was the younger brother of Cameron Flack (MIA) and Charles Flack (wounded) and was the first cousin of Austin Flack (POW). Mike enlisted at age seventeen. His mother and father, Texie and I.K. Flack Jr., were very emotional. Mike took his basic training at Fort Jackson, South Carolina, and attended artillery school at Fort Bliss, Texas, before shipping overseas to Yokohama, Japan, in August of 1951 and receiving posting to the First Cavalry Division. Mike declined the combat exemption that he was due because of a MIA brother. *Courtesy of Corienne Flack and Connie Flack Conner.*

Mike Flack served in the field until November of 1952. He saw much devastation and managed to capture an image of a damaged steam locomotive he saw. This photo represents all the damaged and destroyed transportation systems during the fighting in Korea. *Courtesy of Corienne Flack and Connie Flack Conner.*

Corporal Richard A. Wehrstein, former junior executive with the Armour Company in Chicago, Illinois, served with the Seventh Recon Company, Seventh Infantry Division. He participated in the assault on the Triangle Hill Complex near Kum Kwa, Korea. The battle was fiercely fought for several days and resulted in a victory for the UN forces. *Courtesy of Richard A. Wehrstein.*

Corporal Richard A. Wehrstein received the Combat Infantryman's Badge, the Korean Service Medal with Bronze Service Star and the United Nations Service Medal. Wehrstein retired to Rutherford County and lives in the Bostic area. *Courtesy of Richard A. Wehrstein.*

Frederick Leon Derexson, Company C, Thirty-fourth Infantry Regiment, Twenty-fourth Infantry Division, served his country during the Korean War. He was overseas one year, five months and fifteen days. *Courtesy of Nora Derexson.*

For his services Frederick Leon Derexson received the Korean Service Medal, the National Defense Service Medal and the United Nations Service Medal; his unit received the Republic of Korea Presidential Unit Citation. Fred's brothers Jimmy, Clark and Roger also served in the military. Corporal Derexson was a member of American Legion Post #74 and VFW Post 204. *Courtesy of Nora Derexson.*

Seaman Billy Oscar Goode entered service in November of 1952. He served aboard the USS *Bordelon* (DD-881), a Gearing class destroyer, a U.S. Navy mainstay for over twenty years. Named in honor of USMC Staff Sergeant William J. Bordelon, who received the Medal of Honor posthumously for his bravery during the Battle of Tarawa, the *Bordelon* served in the Mediterranean area with the Sixth Fleet. In December 1953 the *Bordelon* served as one of two presidential guard ships that covered the route of President Eisenhower on his way to the Big Three Conference in Bermuda. *Courtesy of Billy Oscar Goode.*

Seaman Billy Oscar Goode received his discharge in September of 1956. For his services he received the Navy Occupation Service Medal with European Clasp and the National Defense Service Medal. *Courtesy of Billy Oscar Goode.*

Before his induction, Adrien Jervis Arledge served with Hamrick and Jones Law Firm in Rutherfordton. He entered service on January 30, 1951, and served in the Instruction Company CSTR TSESS at Camp Gordon, Georgia. Arledge was a Cryptology Specialist, earned the rank of private first class on July 13, 1951, and received commission as a lieutenant. On December 28, 1951, with his Bachelor of Laws he received assignment to army staff judge advocate. First Lieutenant Arledge received his discharge on September 30, 1953. After his military service, Arledge opened his own law firm in Rutherfordton. *Courtesy of Adrien Jervis Arledge.*

Petty Officer 3/C Palmer Dean Bailey, Rutherford County native, was inducted into the U.S. Navy on June 20, 1952, in Columbia, South Carolina, and was sent to San Diego, California, for twelve weeks of "boot training." Palmer's four-year enlistment included three years, eight months and fifteen days of foreign service. He earned the Good Conduct Ribbon and Medal, the National Defense Service Ribbon and Medal, the Korean Campaign Ribbon and Medal, China Service Ribbon and Medal, United Nations Ribbon and Medal and the National China Service Medal (extended). *Courtesy of Palmer Bailey.*

Petty Officer 3/C Palmer Bailey served aboard the USS *Saint Paul* (CA-73). He boarded ship in San Diego, California, and served thirty-three months at sea. He spent twelve months on Adak Island, Alaska. Entering service on June 20, 1952, and receiving discharge on June 19, 1956, Bailey attained the rank of TE 3. Bailey recalls the shelling of Wonsan Harbor, North Korea. The *Saint Paul* is credited with firing the U.S. Navy's final shore bombardment round on July 27, 1953. *Courtesy of Palmer Bailey.*

Robert Wiley Hamrick enlisted in service on July 22, 1952; prior to his enlistment he had served as a lineman for Southern Bell Telephone Company. Assigned to Company A, Ninth Infantry Regiment, Second Infantry Division, this 6 foot 5, 228-pound infantryman earned for his services the Combat Infantryman's Badge, Good Conduct Medal, Korean Service Medal with two Bronze Service Stars, the United Nations Service Medal, National Defense Service Medal and Commendation Ribbon with Medal Pendant. Upon his discharge, he had attained the rank of sergeant first class. *Courtesy of Martha D. Hamrick.*

Another Rutherford County native who served in the Second Infantry was Harold E. Mayse. Mayse attained the rank of sergeant first class while serving with Battery B, Fifteenth Field Artillery Battalion. Mayse served in Korea for thirteen months beginning on February 29, 1952; all this time his unit was assigned to the Second Infantry Division. Upon his induction, Mayse was serving as a gasoline truck driver for the Henson Timber Products Company in Forest City, North Carolina. For his services he received the Korean Service Medal with three Bronze Service Stars and the United Nations Service Medal. *Courtesy of Harold Edwin Mayse.*

Palmer Bailey went to Korea on two different assignments. He spoke of the emotions attached to gifting Chinese orphans aboard ship; the entire crew of 1,645 participated. The chaplain had a service, and the children received shoes, fruits and candies. Palmer married the lovely Frances Gettys from the Hollis community. Frances, a former teacher, is the sister of five brothers: Jeff, Howard, Emmett, Henry and Kenneth, who all served during the Korean era and are listed elsewhere in this book. *Courtesy of Palmer Bailey.*

This photograph shows Mike Flack with an M-2 .50-caliber machine gun. *Courtesy of Corienne Flack and Connie Flack Conner.*

This photograph shows Corporal Mike Flack (right) and a fellow soldier at the entrance of a bunker. During this period of the Korean War most of the combat soldiers had used a dugout or bunker of this type. *Courtesy of Corienne Flack and Connie Flack Conner.*

Celebrating his May 15, 1952, birthday with a cake is Corporal Mike Flack, Third Infantry Division ("Rock of the Marne"). *Courtesy of Corienne Flack and Connie Flack Conner.*

This postwar photograph shows Sergeant First Class Mike Flack (front). He is drilling members of Company K, 3rd Battalion, 323rd Infantry Regiment (a North Carolina National Guard Unit) at Fort Jackson, South Carolina, on July 12, 1965. Shown here are Sergeant First Class Earl C. Stott (Forest City, North Carolina), Sergeant First Class Donald L. Tate (Forest City, North Carolina), Sergeant First Class Charles R. Norville (Rutherfordton, North Carolina) and Staff Sargeant William L. Long. The 323rd is on two weeks active duty training at Fort Jackson, South Carolina. *Courtesy of Corienne Flack and Connie Flack Conner.*

Forest City native Howard M. Smith served with the Service Company, Fourth Infantry Division ("Ivy") at Ladd Air Force Base in Alaska—quite a change from Fort Jackson, where he received his basic training. Howard distinctly remembered this photograph because the rubber band on his right pant leg had just broken. Here he stands in front of a winterized two and a half-ton truck. *Courtesy of Howard M. Smith.*

Howard M. Smith remembers that the snow in Alaska was often so dry that "you could not even make a snowball out of it." Howard remarked to the authors that after serving in Alaska, he was glad to get out of service. Howard Smith earned the National Defense Service Medal and the Good Conduct Medal. *Courtesy of Howard M. Smith.*

Cliffside native Lee Garvin Edney served between May 3, 1951, and April 4, 1953. He attained the rank of corporal while serving in the Eightieth Engineer Company (DEPOT). He received assignments in both Germany and France. *Courtesy of Grace Edney Quick.*

Lee Garvin Edney was married to Grace Edney until his untimely death in an automobile accident on December 14, 2000. *Courtesy of Grace Edney Quick.*

Walter Boyce Crowder, son of Lee and Winnie Crowder, began serving in Korea on March 10, 1952. Boyce had had basic training at Fort George C. Meade in Maryland. His advanced training was at Fort Leonard Wood in Missouri. His assignment was to Company B, 430th Construction Engineer Battalion. After his fourteen-day voyage across the Pacific Ocean, he went ashore at Inchon. During his tour in Korea he went from north of the thirty-eighth parallel down to Pusan. Here he holds his M-1 Garand rifle with bayonet fixed. *Courtesy of Walter Crowder and Susie Byers.*

Walter Boyce Crowder attained the rank of corporal and recalled, "Korea was a country torn apart by war." Crowder had many buddies—some of whom did not get to return home. He left the front line on January 21, 1953, when "it was only seventeen below zero. I got to ride back in an open truck for thirty-five miles." From there, Crowder went to Pusan and back to Japan; he traveled on the *General Hase* for fourteen days to San Francisco. *Courtesy of Walter Crowder and Susie Byers.*

When Walter Boyce Crowder received his discharge at Fort Jackson on February 19, 1953, he and his buddy Alex Beam hired a taxi for twenty-five dollars to take them to Forest City after "stopping at the first liquor store on the way." Crowder says, "I was proud and glad to give two years of my life for my country." His daughter Susie was born on September 21, 1954. *Courtesy of Walter Crowder and Susie Byers.*

Private First Class Thomas P. Tisdale III, Rutherford County native, entered service in December of 1952. After twelve weeks at Forth Jackson, he was assigned to Company L, Fourteenth Infantry Regiment, Twenty-fifth Infantry Division. Tisdale sailed from Seattle to Japan. *Courtesy of Thomas P. Tisdale IV.*

Private First Class Thomas P. Tisdale III vividly recalled receiving a series of inoculations before his deployment to Korea from Japan. He remembered his entry into Korea through Inchon. *Courtesy of Thomas P. Tisdale IV.*

Private First Class Thomas P. Tisdale III served with his division for about ten months in Korea. Foxholes, trenches and bunkers were not unusual sights to PFC Tisdale. For his services Tisdale earned the Combat Infantryman's Badge, the Korean Service Medal and the National Defense Service Medal. *Courtesy of Thomas P. Tisdale IV.*

This communion photograph in the collection of Private First Class Thomas P. Tisdale III is a very moving image of combat life. A very active member of Bethel Baptist Church of Ellenboro, North Carolina, Tisdale would have observed and preserved this sacred moment. *Courtesy of Thomas P. Tisdale IV.*

Thomas P. Tisdale III married Jean Green Tisdale. Thomas P. Tisdale III, the self-proclaimed "Prettiest Man in Ellenboro," was a local merchant and radio announcer. Jean, the author of *Dear Companion* and *Forward Through the Ages: A History of Bethel Baptist Church*, an organist for her church for half a century, active club member and mother of Thomas P. Tisdale IV, Pam Tisdale McFarland and Cathy Tisdale Murray, still found time to work in the store. Jean's heroic battle with cancer was an inspiration to the authors' mothers—both of whom fought that battle also. *Courtesy of Thomas P. Tisdale IV.*

The Spring and Summer of 1953

SPRING 1953–JULY 26, 1953

The spring of 1953 would bring CCF attacks on the Eighth Army's outpost lines. By July 1953 these attacks would reach an intensity comparable to the intensity of the attacks of 1951. The UN and South Korean troops numbered 768,000 in opposition to the 800,000 Chinese and North Koreans. There were more than 1.5 million troops on the Korean Peninsula. Confrontations, however, were at a minimum during this period.

March brought an increase in enemy attacks on the Second Infantry Division, Seventh Infantry Division and First Marine Regiment. The CCF managed several successful ambushes during March 9–10 of 1953.

Operation Little Switch was the exchange of the sick and wounded POWs. The operation began on April 20 and was completed by the latter part of the month; 684 UN prisoners were exchanged for more than 6,000 Communist detainees.

Throughout April negotiations resumed. The POW question was settled by providing each side an opportunity to persuade those captives who refused repatriation to change their minds.

May 1953 saw the Twenty-fifth Infantry Division inflict over 3,200 casualties on the CCF when it attacked three divisional outposts. By June 18 the armistice was all but complete, but Syngman Rhee thwarted the final signing by releasing more than 25,000 North Korean anti-Communist POWs. The North Korean officials considered this release a breach of faith; his actions delayed the final signing for another month during which some of the fiercest fighting of the war occurred. July casualties for the CCF totaled no less than 72,000.

Some of the continuing major battles of the Korean War focused on such positions as Outpost Harry, Pork Chop Hill and Old Baldy. These names and the continued fighting there have become almost synonymous with the Korean War. In fact, Hollywood later capitalized on these battles by producing such films as *Pork Chop Hill*, starring Gregory Peck, and *M*A*S*H*, starring Donald Sutherland and Robert Duvall.

One of the service personnel participating in the blood fighting at Pork Chop Hill was Rutherford County native Ben Evans Wall Jr. Sergeant Wall was a member of the Eighty-second Anti-Aircraft Artillery Battalion, attached to the Second Infantry Division. *Courtesy of Ben Evans Wall Jr.*

This photograph during a lull in the recent fighting on Old Baldy (March of 1953) shows Ben Evans Wall Jr. *Courtesy of Ben Evans Wall Jr.*

Ben Evans Wall Jr. participated in fighting not only at Old Baldy but also at Pork Chop Hill. *Courtesy of Ben Evans Wall Jr.*

Here, Ben Evans Wall Jr. stands beside a quad .50-caliber anti-aircraft machine gun mounted on a half-track.
Courtesy of Ben Evans Wall Jr.

Ben Evans Wall Jr. labeled this image as "Skyline." This photograph shows the typical terrain near the front. *Courtesy of Ben Evans Wall Jr.*

Ben Evans Wall Jr. contributed this frontline photograph of a position near T-Bone to the book *Rutherford County and the Korean War*; Wall has kept this image for half a century. *Courtesy of Ben Evans Wall Jr.*

This photograph preserves the firing of the 666,666[th] round of artillery. *Courtesy of Ben Evans Wall Jr.*

Caroleen native Broadus Lee Quinn joined the U.S. Army at the age of nineteen. His assignment was Company I, Twenty-third Infantry Regiment, Second Infantry Division ("Warriors"). *Courtesy of Lee Quinn.*

Ben Evans Wall Jr. suffered wounds during his service and ended up in the 382nd General Hospital at Gifu, Japan. Wall captured the image of these enlisted personnel feeding deer near Nara, Japan. Because of his wounds, Ben Evans Wall Jr. earned the Purple Heart Medal; he was also entitled to the National Defense Service Medal, the Korean Service Medal with three Bronze Service Stars and the United Nation Service Medal. *Courtesy of Ben Evans Wall Jr.*

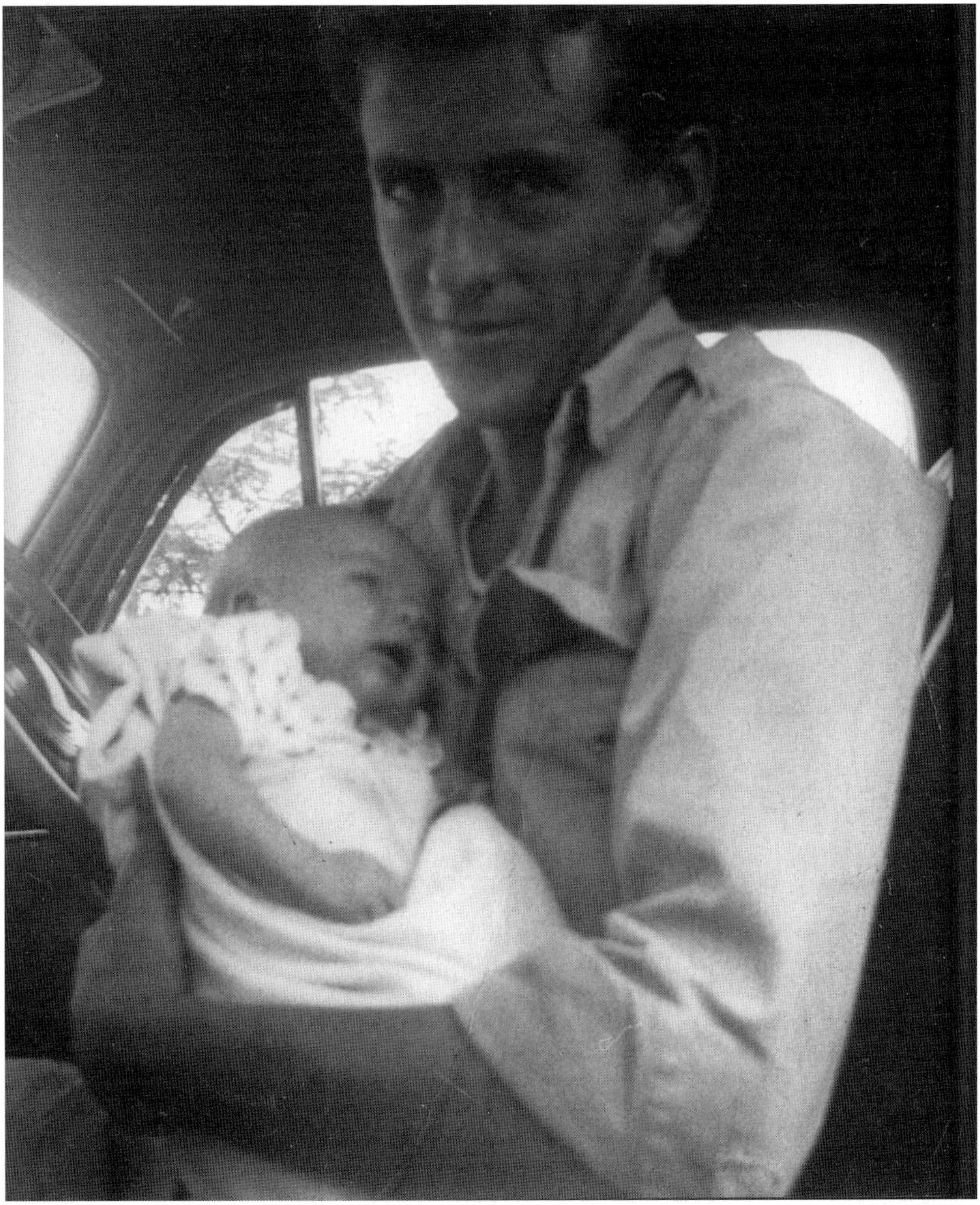

Here Edward Wallace Crook tenderly holds his daughter Donna Crook in the cab of their Ford truck. For his services in Korea, Edward received the Purple Heart Medal, the Combat Infantryman's Badge (with the Seventeenth Infantry Regiment, Seventh Infantry Division), the Korean Service Medal with Bronze Service Star, the United Nations Service Medal and the National Defense Service Medal. *Courtesy of Donna Crook.*

Corporal Edward Wallace Crook served in the United States Army with Headquarters and Headquarters Detachment, Eighth Transportation Battalion (Helicopter). Edward Crook participated in the Battle of Pork Chop Hill and was wounded in that battle in 1953. Here he (left) and his brother Ernest William Crook pose together. Both served in the United States Army. *Courtesy of Donna Crook.*

Infantryman Broadus Lee Quinn recalls the coldness of the winter and the heat of the summer. He served for one month on Koje-Do Island at one of the POW camps; it was so cold in 1952, Quinn recalled, that he took his sleeping bag to wrap up with in the watchtower. In 1953, Lee Quinn and other members of the Second Infantry Division were on the front line; they conducted numerous patrols and participated in the battle of Old Baldy. *Courtesy of Lee Quinn.*

Sergeant First Class Quinn is pictured here with his friend and ROK soldier Joh Jin Deuk. Joh was a KATUSA assigned to Quinn. *Courtesy of Lee Quinn.*

Corporal Samuel Chivous Waters was trained on light infantry weapons. During his service in Korea, he participated in the fighting at Monk's Hood and Pork Chop Hill. *Courtesy of Samuel Chivous Waters.*

This photograph shows Corporal Samuel Chivous Waters in Korea. During his time there, he was captured but managed to escape. He is pictured here as a young man with a bazooka beside him; the sand bags are near a communication trench. *Courtesy of Samuel Chivous Waters.*

Like other members of the Second Infantry Division, Corporal Samuel Chivous Waters had a KATUSA assigned to him. Pictured here with Sam Waters is his friend Goolsby. *Courtesy of Samuel Chivous Waters.*

Being a Rutherford County lad, Corporal Samuel Chivous Waters was familiar with the pick and demonstrated his skill on occasion. Waters remembers being at the DMZ at the signing of the truce. Waters's trench was on the south side on this glad day. *Courtesy of Samuel Chivous Waters.*

Also serving in the Second Infantry Division was Corporal Samuel Chivous Waters, a Rutherford County native. Samuel Chivous Waters served in Company E, Twenty-eighth Infantry Regiment, Second Infantry Division. His tour of duty was from November 7, 1952, through November 6, 1954. *Courtesy of Samuel Chivous Waters.*

For his services, Corporal Samuel Chivous Waters received the Combat Infantryman's Badge, the Korean Service Medal with Bronze Star, the United Nations Service Medal, the National Defense Service Medal and the Good Conduct Medal. After the war, Samuel Chivous Waters worked at the Stonecutter Mill for twenty-five years. He remembered being paid in silver dollars one Christmas. Waters served as a deputy sheriff with the Rutherford County Sheriff's Department for seventeen years. *Courtesy of Samuel Chivous Waters.*

Staff Sergeant Elish Lynch "E.L." Whiteside entered service January 20, 1953. He remembered his good times "running around Green Hill" with his cousin Bryant Womack, who would later become a Medal of Honor recipient. In July 1953 Whiteside, Company I, Fifteenth Infantry Regiment, Third Infantry Division, was wounded in Korea by CCF mortar fire, transported to Japan and hospitalized for his recovery. Whiteside earned the Purple Heart Medal, Good Conduct Medal, Korean Service Medal with Bronze Service Star, United Nations Service Medal and National Defense Service Medal. *Courtesy of E.L. Whiteside.*

Henry Decator Gettys of Hollis was one of five Gettys brothers (Kenneth, Howard, Jefferson and James Emmett) who served in the U.S. military. The son of Zeno and Vera Gettys, he enlisted in April of 1951. This portrait of Henry shows him in dress uniform. Sergeant First Class Henry Gettys shared his strongest memories in a newspaper interview: going to the front line, sleeping on the ground in the trenches, sleeping under a tent only once, enduring temperatures during the winter of minus thirty degrees Fahrenheit and below, nightmares after his return home and looking for a foxhole upon hearing a loud noise. *Courtesy of Frances Gettys Bailey.*

Henry Gettys, in front of the family home, trained at Fort Hood, Texas, for the Armored Infantry. Gettys had worked with the U.S. Coast and Geodetic Survey and credited this outdoor living and work as helping him survive in Korea. In February 1953 a fragment of white phosphorous from an exploding mortar shell in the fighting around Old Baldy wounded Henry. Intense fighting prevented Gettys's evacuation. White phosphorous is non-extinguishable by water and the burn increased. Henry held a tomato to the burn to relieve the pain. He was taken to Japan for recuperation in March 1953. *Courtesy of Frances Gettys Bailey.*

Corporal Waters was not present when this 1984 photo was made, but it does show his colleagues, one of whom was Nell Daves Price Burns (first row, fifth from left), the mother of one of the authors of this book. *Front, left to right:* "Rasta," L.M. Boone, "Gracie." *First Row:* Sheriff Damon Huskey; Chief Russell Duncan; Captain Ray Dixon; Secretary Chris Epley; recorder Nell Burns; Deputies Ruby Waters and Denise Baker; dispatchers Mary Jo Barnhill, Kim Hensley and Katrina Mock; First Lieutenant C.W. Simmons; Lieutenants Keith Dobbins and Ronnie McCombs; *Second Row:* Lieutenants Luke Roberson, Charles Conner, Mike Summers and Ken Thomas; Sergeants Bill Ives, Herbert Scruggs, David Petty and Ron Fish; *Third Row:* Jailors Don Johnston and Leon Greene; Deputies Bill Watts, James Owens, Harvey McDaniel, Barry Horne, Randy Lee, Bill Harper and Terry Moore; *Fourth Row:* Crime prevention Hoover Conner; jailor Don Casner; maintenance David Hill; Deputies Don Price and Roger Maxwell. *Not pictured:* Lieutenant James Sparks, dietician Peggy Hill and Deputy Sam Waters. *Courtesy of Anita Price Davis.*

James Emmett Gettys was the only one of the five Gettys brothers to serve in the United States Navy. Emmett enlisted just after his graduation in May of 1951. Fireman 3/C James Emmett Gettys served aboard the USS *Kenneth D. Bailey* (DD-713), a Gearing class destroyer. Emmett Gettys was in the U.S. Navy from 1951 until 1955. He trained at Bainbridge, Maryland, and completed firefighting school at Newport, Rhode Island. He was in France, Italy, Turkey and Spain during his career. The USS *Kenneth D. Bailey* had the misfortune of losing a man overboard during a storm near Guantanamo. *Courtesy of Emmett Gettys.*

Corporal Howard Alexander Gettys, one of the five Gettys brothers who served in the 1950s, entered service in January 1951 and received his discharge in January 1953. He was stationed in Germany and served with the Sixty-sixth Engineer Topographical Company. In his civilian life Howard Gettys had been a surveyor. He received additional training at the Engineer's School, Fort Belvoir, Virginia. Howard earned the Occupation Medal (Germany). Howard's younger brother Jefferson finished two years at Appalachian State before his service career sent him to Germany in 1954; Jefferson appears in the last chapter of this book. *Courtesy of Howard A. Gettys.*

Kenneth W. Gettys enlisted in the United States Army in 1950 just before graduation from Hollis High School. Sergeant First Class Kenneth Gettys, Thirteenth Combat Engineers, Thirty-first Infantry Regiment, Seventh Infantry Division ("Bayonet"), served seven years, eleven months and twenty-one days with two thirteen-month tours in Korea. He participated with his unit in battles at Iron Triangle Hills, Old Baldy, Heartbreak Ridge and the Punch Bowl. When his sister Frances asked him what he did in service, he said, "I did what I was told and tried to stay alive." This photo was made in Seoul in 1952. Kenneth Gettys earned the Purple Heart Medal with Oak Leaf Cluster, Korean Service Medal with two Bronze Service Stars, the United Nations Service Medal, the National Defense Service Medal and the Good Conduct Medal (twice). Kenneth Gettys served as a crane operator with Daniel Construction Company for thirty-four years without an unexcused absence. When Kenneth's wife Polly submitted Kenneth's military photo that he had sent home from Seoul in 1952, she commented in the enclosure, "Wasn't he a handsome nineteen-year-old?" Polly went on to say, "World War II and the Korean War affected thousands of lives. Wars are not just statistics. Young men are trained to kill; they see death firsthand. War changes them forever." *Courtesy of Kenneth Gettys and Frances Gettys Bailey.*

John Samuel Metcalf, Rutherford County native, joined the U.S. Air Force on January 6, 1953. He received training as a supply clerk, and he served with the 308th Armt&Elect Main Squadron (Strategic Air Command). *Courtesy of John Samuel Metcalf.*

During his tour of duty Staff Sergeant Metcalf had stations in Newbury, England; Morocco; and Hunter Air Force Base, Savannah, Georgia. For his service he received the Good Conduct Medal and the National Defense Service Medal. After his tour of duty, he graduated from Furman in 1961. A business major, he worked afterwards at Wachovia, at Spindale Mills, as a teacher and as a vocational counselor. *Courtesy of John Samuel Metcalf.*

In this recent photo of John S. Metcalf, he wears a cap given to him by his beloved grandchildren, Savannah Parton and Christopher Wellmon. The cap identifies him as the "Top Pop." *Courtesy of John Samuel Metcalf.*

Career sailor Wilbur J. Burgin entered the service May 6, 1943, and retired August 1, 1974. Captain Burgin recalled spending four years in the Mediterranean on destroyers, earning his wings in October of 1950, serving aboard several different carriers and in various air groups, serving in propeller-driven aircraft until 1956, and transitioning into jets. He served as commanding officer of a jet squadron, as an "Air Boss" on another carrier and as an aide to an admiral. During his career Captain Burgin had over five thousand flight hours and over five hundred carrier landings. *Courtesy of Wilbur J. Burgin.*

Captain Wilbur J. Burgin (U.S. Navy, Retired) helped open the Rutherford County Farm Museum in July of 1994 at 240 Depot Street in the J.W. Davis Building in Forest City, North Carolina. The state-incorporated museum, which allows deductions for donated items, is open for visitors. Displays include farm implements, hand-sewn items and even washing machines. The museum welcomes your donations and loans. *Courtesy of Wilbur J. Burgin and Bob Morgan.*

Radioman 3/C Delbert Edgar "D.E" Byars entered the U.S. Navy in April 1948, went to San Diego for twelve weeks of "boot training" and completed sixteen weeks of radioman school before being transferred to Guam, where he served twenty-four months. Byars served on the USS *Tranthen* (DD-539), a Navy destroyer being re-commissioned. He was training new recruits on adjusting to shipboard life at his discharge; he received recommendation for re-enlistment. D.E. married Helen McKinney Byars; they attended the 2005 Veteran's Day Celebration at the National Guard Armory. *Courtesy of D.E. Byars and James M. Walker.*

Master Sergeant Rodney Joseph Beauchamp, twenty-three-year U.S. Marine veteran, served with the First, Second and Third Marine Divisions in Korea, Germany, Norway, Russia, Okinawa, Japan, Vietnam, Philippines and Camp Lejeune, North Carolina. He earned the Good Conduct Medal, Korean Service Medal with Bronze Service Star, United Nations Service Medal, National Defense Service Medal, Korean Presidential Unit Citation, Navy Occupational Service Medal with European Clasp, the Vietnamese Meritorious Civil Actions Color with Palm and Frame, Navy Unit Commendation and Vietnamese Meritorious Unit Citation Gallantry Cross with Bronze Service Star. *Courtesy of Rodney Joseph Beauchamp and James M. Walker.*

Corporal Herman Taylor served his entire enlistment at Fort Riley, Kansas, where he was assigned to Company H, Eighty-fifth Infantry Regiment, Thirty-seventh Division. Corporal Taylor was a driver for an 81 millimeter mortar team. Before he entered service, Taylor was an instrument man with the Cook Electric Company in Chicago. Born in Spindale, Corporal Taylor earned the National Defense Service Medal. *Courtesy of Tammy Harrill.*

John B. Ledbetter of the Lake Lure community had been a member of the Mount Nebo Baptist Church of Lake Lure. He was a 1949 graduate of Johnson C. Smith. He was drafted on November 29, 1950, and trained at Fort Jackson, South Carolina. He was sent to Japan on May 16, 1951. *Courtesy of Ruth Ledbetter Freeman.*

John B. Ledbetter was killed in action on September 11, 1951. His parents (Mr. and Mrs. Burgin Ledbetter), five sisters and one brother survived him. His sister Ruth remarked to the authors, "He gave his life for his country." *Courtesy of Ruth Ledbetter Freeman.*

Clifford W. Conner was a third class builder who served from 1951 to 1955. He recalls his ship, the USS *Henrico* APA-45. He helped in troop transport from November of 1951 until March of 1952. While in the Seabees, Conner helped in loading ordnance on six ships bound for Korea. Here he shares some "off time" aboard ship with a buddy. *Courtesy of Clifford W. Conner.*

Rutherford County resident Clifford W. Conner served in both the U.S. Navy and the Seabees over a four-year period in the 1950s. *Courtesy of Clifford W. Conner.*

Conner served in Virginia, Japan and Korea. He still remembered the tidal differences at Inchon. His stations also included Newfoundland and Cuba, where his unit built a warehouse. Despite his dedicated service, he still found time to challenge some fish. *Courtesy of Clifford W. Conner.*

Private First Class Paige N. Jones, who served in the Fifty-fourth Engineers with the Eighth Army, was familiar with the Inchon area. Jones constructed a diorama of the Inchon area and brought it and other service mementos to the 2005 Veteran's Day Celebration on November 11, 2005, at the Hobart Daniel Armory. *Courtesy of Paige N. Jones and James M. Walker.*

PFC Jones recalled a varied career in the military. Private First Class Paige N. Jones served his nation from 1953 until 1961. Upon his Honorable Discharge, he earned the Korean Service Medal, the United Nations Service Medal, the National Defense Service Medal and the Good Conduct Medal. *Courtesy of Paige N. Jones.*

During his one year in Korea, Burwell found time to photograph Korea and its people. Here John poses with his KATUSA, Mr. Kim; pictured with them is Kim's child. Kim worked in the same office as John. *Courtesy of John Burwell.*

Private First Class Curtis M. Smawley, graduate of Harris High School, was working in Detroit at the Chrysler Corporation as a final assembler when he received his draft notice. Assigned to Company L, 279th Infantry Regiment, Eighth Army, he served in Korea as a military policeman. Smawley served overseas one year, five months and twenty days. For his services he earned the Combat Infantryman's Badge, the Korean Service Medal and the United National Defense Service Medal. *Courtesy of Charles A. Rich.*

Corporal John Burwell served in the United States Army, arriving in Korea from Japan on July 27, 1953. Corporal Burwell was assigned to the provost's office in Inchon; his duty was chief clerk. Here Corporal Burwell is at his duty station. *Courtesy of John Burwell.*

Among the subjects of John Burwell's 1953 photographs was a child in traditional clothes. The child (center, front) is wearing a jacket of bright yellow material, a skirt of flaming red, little white rubber shoes and white socks. *Courtesy of John Burwell.*

This view of typical Korean housing shows the difficult conditions that the Koreans endured at the war's end. The bicycle leaning against the house is indicative of a common means of transportation. The rickshaw was a popular way of travel. *Courtesy of John Burwell.*

Here the grain market is evident in another 1953 photograph belonging to John Burwell. The grain sold by the traditionally clad residents was generally rice. *Courtesy of John Burwell.*

As Crawley got on the ship for overseas, the armistice was signed. Crawley recalled that they still had to be on guard because they were exchanging prisoners. Here C.B. Crawley Jr. (right) pauses with a buddy to smile for the camera. The unwelcoming terrain is evident in the background. *Courtesy of Mary Crawley.*

C.B. Crawley Jr., Henrietta native, served in the United States Army from 1952 until 1954. *Courtesy of Mary Crawley.*

Private C.B. Crawley Jr.'s duty entailed hauling ammunition. Here he demonstrates a camouflage technique. For his services he would receive the Good Conduct Medal and the National Defense Service Medal. *Courtesy of Mary Crawley.*

The War is Over

JULY 27, 1953

Finally, both sides reached an agreement and signed an armistice on July 27, 1953. By the terms of the armistice, a line of demarcation between North and South Korea approximated the front line at the final hour of the war. Three days after the signing of the armistice, the opposing forces withdrew two kilometers on each side of the line to establish a demilitarized zone. In 2006, this demilitarized zone still marks the border between North and South Korea.

The Korean War casualties for the North Korean and Chinese Communist Forces totaled approximately 600,000 dead. The UN command deaths amounted to about 475,000. There are no accurate records of civilian casualties.

Brothers Bobby Glenn Russell (who entered service on January 20, 1953, and was discharged on December 15, 1954) and Dupree Russell both served during the Korean War. The two boys served in different companies in Korea. *Courtesy of Virginia Russell.*

Bobby Glenn Russell served with the 505th Quartermaster RCLM and MAINT Company, 501st Quartermaster Battalion, I Corps. Corporal Russell and the other members of the battalion constructed a four-room building to replace the war-torn school used by four hundred children of the village of Uijongbu, Korea. *Courtesy of Virginia Russell.*

Corporal Russell returned to the United States and his parents (Mr. and Mrs. Ralph Russell) aboard the USNS *General M.B. Stewart* (T-AP 140). *Courtesy of Virginia Russell.*

James Clarence Burns of Ellenboro was inducted into service on the same day that Bobby Glenn Russell entered service. James, a 1950 graduate of Ellenboro High School, later married Peggy Pace (Burns). Shortly after his service, James opened his own business, Burns's Garage, in Ellenboro. *Courtesy of Ellenboro Treasure Chest (1950).*

Interestingly, drill instructor Kenneth Levi Burns (the brother of James Clarence Burns) was in service for a while at the same time as his brother. Kenneth served in Okinawa and completed twelve years with the army. He worked with ordnance during his military career. *Courtesy of Kenneth and Beverly Burns.*

A 1953 graduate of Ellenboro High School, Kenneth Levi Burns was very diverse; he was a member of the annual staff, the drama club, the glee club and the Future Farmers of America. After his military service, he worked with Duke Power Company as a computer specialist; his co-workers described him as "brilliant." Kenneth Burns was very proud of his son (who bears his name) and of his namesake's wife (Beverly); the young couple resides in Ellenboro near Kenneth's childhood home. *Courtesy of Ellenboro Treasure Chest (1953) and Bud Crow.*

After Corporal Joseph E. Ford's capture on February 13, 1951, he remained a POW for two and a half years. His release came on August 13, 1953. Ford recalled to the authors that when he arrived home, "I was one more hungry boy." *Courtesy of Joseph E. Ford.*

When Ford arrived in the county, numerous activities had been planned to celebrate his homecoming. Among these events on his first day home was the Hendersonville Apple Festival Parade of 1953. He particularly remembers the kiss planted on his cheek by the Apple Queen Lib Carnegie, who was also serving as Miss Rutherford County at that time. *Courtesy of Joseph E. Ford.*

The media, family and friends gathered to welcome Ford home. Pictured here are his sister Sarah (first on left, front row), his mother Mary Moffitt Ford (at Sarah's shoulder), Joe Ford (in uniform) and father Noah E. Ford (far right, front row). Corporal Joseph E. Ford received the Combat Infantryman's Badge, POW Medal, National Defense Service Medal, Korean Service Medal and United Nations Service Medal. Joe Ford attended Harris Veteran School at Harris High School, where veterans could complete their high school program. Mr. Worth Lewis, the principal, led this operation. *Courtesy of Joseph E. Ford.*

Three POWs from Rutherford County were honored on that glad day. These joyous men were (left to right) Joseph E. Ford, Austin D. Flack and Pharris Green. Flack, the first person from the county captured in the Korean War, would spend 1,143 days in captivity before his release on August 19, 1953. *Courtesy of Joseph E. Ford.*

Robert "Bob" Humphries remained in service after his release and repatriation on August 20, 1953. He would go on to serve in Vietnam before retiring in 1972. For his services in Korea and Vietnam, Humphries received nine separate decorations, including the Bronze Star Medal, the POW Medal, Good Conduct Medal, United Nations Korean Service Medal and the Korean Service Medal, among others. *Courtesy of Ray Humphries and the* Gastonia Gazette.

Humphries's military career overlapped with another Southerner who knew poverty. Shown here is the young Elvis Presley with Sergeant Humphries. Elvis had entered service on March 24, 1958, after receiving his draft notice. He had entered the U.S. Army from Memphis, Tennessee. Sergeant Presley received his discharge at Fort Dix, New Jersey, on March 5, 1960. Bob now resides in the Kings Mountain area. *Courtesy of Willie Mae Plemmons and Ray Humphries.*

On September 5, 1953, after 1,013 days of captivity, Corporal Bailey Gillespie and others were marched to Panmunjon. Bailey weighed less than 100 pounds, as compared to his former 170 pounds. He sailed home on the U.S. Navy ship *R.L. Howze.* Here, North Carolina Senator Jesse Helms has just presented Bailey with the Purple Heart Medal. Bailey also earned the Good Conduct Medal, National Defense Service Medal, Korean Service Medal with Four Bronze Service Stars, the United Nations Service Medal, the Occupation Medal (Japan), the POW Medal and the Combat Medical Badge. *Courtesy of Bailey and Joy Gillespie,* Korean War Remembered.

Unfortunately, not all Rutherford County men returned home. Cameron Flack, L Company, Third Battalion, Thirty-first Infantry Regiment, Seventh Infantry Division, had been missing since December 12, 1950, when CC forces attacked his unit; there was a "presumptive find of death in 1953." In 2005 remains from the Chosin Reservoir areas arrived in Hawaii. Through the publicity of Jean Gordon, the *Daily Courier*, WLOS, Mary Jedlicka, the *Asheville Citizen Times*, and the North Carolina American Legion (especially Billy Seay and Jack Nanney), families knew to submit DNA samples. The DNA of Cameron Flack's family members (especially sister Shirley Flack Mace) helped to identify his remains, and he received posthumous promotion to sergeant. Families' DNA samples also positively identified Lolan Bridges and Thomas Wray Yelton. *Courtesy of Corienne Flack and Connie Flack Conner.*

A Rutherford County native who remembers well the prisoner exchange is Corporal Samuel A. Harrison. Harrison served as Honor Guard during the tense, emotional exchange. *Courtesy of Samuel A. Harrison.*

Serving in Korea, Corporal Samuel A. Harrison remembers well the rugged terrain and the extreme temperatures that marked the Korean peninsula. His most vivid memory was serving in the Forward Observation Post when five thousand Chinese Communist troops "came across" and he was able to call it in to our artillery. *Courtesy of Samuel A. Harrison.*

Corporal Samuel A. Harrison served in Headquarters Company, 936th Field Artillery Battalion. Harrison proudly served his country in the diverse duties it required of him. After the truce, Corporal Samuel A. Harrison helped establish important communication lines. High above the ground, Harrison proudly performs his duties with competence and the good cheer expected of him from birth. *Courtesy of Samuel A. Harrison.*

Here, Corporal Samuel A. Harrison and Sergeant Tripplett confront "a problem" on a day in the field. *Courtesy of Samuel A. Harrison.*

For his services, Corporal Samuel A. Harrison received the National Defense Service Medal, the United Nations Service Medal and the Good Conduct Medal. *Courtesy of Samuel A. Harrison.*

James Myron Shows served in Company I, Fourteenth Armored Cavalry Regiment, Seventh Army. He received his basic training at Fort Jackson, South Carolina; his advanced training was at the Army Chemical Center in Edgewood, Maryland. *Courtesy of James M. Shows.*

Trooper James Myron Shows attained the rank of corporal while teaching biological warfare in Badhersfield, Germany. He coached the KSLI (King's Shropshire Light Infantry) in basketball in the British zone of occupation in Berlin; his team won the basketball championship between the various battalions. Shows earned the Good Conduct Medal, the National Defense Service Medal and the Army of Occupation (Germany). This 1954 photograph pictures Shows on a field exercise; he is posed beside his track and is holding his weapon. *Courtesy of James M. Shows.*

Second Lieutenant Nancy Hardwick Jones enlisted in active service in the United States Air Force on December 11, 1953. Lieutenant Jones served in the military personnel office. She had previously completed training for clerk typist, recruiting and Air Force Administration. She served overseas at the Chateau Roux Air Depot in France. *Courtesy of Nancy Hardwick Jones.*

Yeoman Seaman Betty Sue Taylor attended Yeoman "A" School, where she took courses in filing, service record entries, correspondence, GTC for Pos and other duties. She enlisted at Spartanburg, South Carolina, on August 15, 1955. Betty Sue Taylor served with Flag Allowance, Commander in Chief, Pacific Fleet (CINCPACFLT). Here she appears at her swearing-in ceremony. Betty Sue Taylor remains active in veteran affairs and serves her community with dignity. *Courtesy of Betty Sue Taylor.*

County resident Namond Earl McComas served in the United States Air Force from 1952 to 1956. Airman Third Class McComas had duty in Texas, France and at Larson Air Force Base in Moses Lake, Washington. During his tour he served as a vehicle operator. He earned the National Defense Service Medal. McComas continues to serve the veterans in Rutherford County and to participate in veteran affairs. *Courtesy of Namond Earl McComas.*

Seaman Bobby William Laughter served in the United States Navy. He was at Orange Naval Station at Orange, Texas. He served at the Subic Bay Naval Station, Philippine Islands. His term of service was from March 15, 1951, until March 14, 1955. He retired from Yelton Milling Company and then went to work as a salesman for Marketing Specialist. He married Frances Taylor (Spindale). They have one daughter, Crystal Horn of Ellenboro, and two granddaughters. They are active in the First Baptist Church of Spindale. His father is Roscoe Laughter, who was ninety-four at the time of this writing. *Courtesy of Bobby William Laughter.*

Duncan's Creek native, Specialist Third Joe Price served with Headquarters and Service Company, ARMAV Regiment, at Fort Rucker, Alabama. His training specialty was Tandem Rotor Helicopter Mechanic for the H-19 "Flying Banana" helicopter. He also received training at the transportation school for sixteen weeks. Joe received the National Defense Service Medal. *Courtesy of Joe Price and Billy Seay.*

Here Joe Price is explaining details of a helicopter transmission to his superiors. Upon his discharge, Joe Price received glowing letters of appreciation concerning his excellence of service. His lieutenant colonel wrote about the excellent manner in which Joe performed his assigned duties and said that his departure was a loss to the army; his superior officer also commented upon Joe's attitude, which helped Joe get along and work in harmony with his associates. *Courtesy of Joe Price and Billy Seay.*

Another Rutherford County resident who received excellent commendations was Billie W. Childers, a Caroleen native who served in the Air Force. Airman First Childers served in the 839th Combat Engineers, 18th Fighter-Bomber Wing, Fifth Air Force. Childers's unit was tasked with improving the K-55 Air Field at Osan, South Korea. The improvements included construction of water filtration plants and billets for the troops and reinforcement and lengthening runaways. This photograph shows the construction site of K-55 of Osan, South Korea. *Courtesy of Billie W. Childers.*

Without pure water, the personnel on Base K-55 could not have existed. This photo shows two 2 ½-ton trucks equipped with water tanks on their rear. The tanks are being filled at the water filtration system. *Courtesy of Billie W. Childers.*

This view shows two F-84 jets being serviced inside their revetment, which is a wall or barrier that protects the aircraft from hostile strafing and bombing. Base K-55 was also home to F-86 Saberjets. The base was home to the Eighteenth Fighter-Bomber Wing. Base K-55 was located in the valley between Hill 170 and Hill 180 near Osan. *Courtesy of Billie W. Childers.*

Billie W. Childers had received special training at the Army Engineering School at Fort Belvoir, Virginia. His tender side shows as he sits on a sandbag revetment with a Korean child. *Courtesy of Billie W. Childers.*

This photograph shows the billet upgrading at K-55 from tents to Quonset huts. These improved living quarters for base personnel provided warmer living areas during the harsh Korean winters, where temperatures could drop below minus forty degrees Fahrenheit. *Courtesy of Billie W. Childers.*

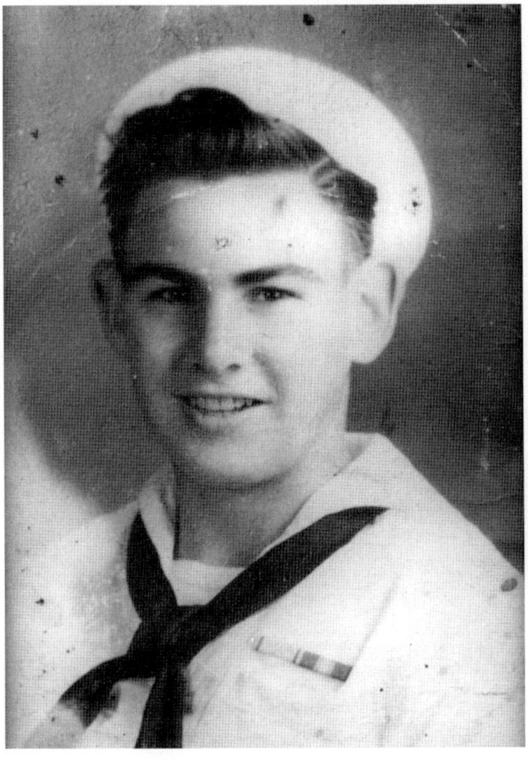

Gunner's Mate 3/C James Melton Chapman of Caroleen served from August of 1954 through June of 1955. *Courtesy of Dorothy Chapman.*

Chapman served aboard the USS *Isherwood (DD520)* Chapman was in charge of a five-inch turret. For his services he received the China Service Medal (Extended), the National Defense Service Medal and the Good Conduct Medal. *Courtesy of Dorothy Chapman.*

The navy has long maintained its tradition of holding King Neptune's Court to initiate polliwogs who cross the equator. Sailors of all rank who had never made the crossing before would be forced to humiliate themselves before the King Neptune. In the above photograph the "Queen" is Gunner's Mate Chapman. *Courtesy of Dorothy Chapman.*

Corporal James Alvin Bennett, 822nd Engineers Aviation Battalion and Medical Company, Sixty-first Infantry Regiment, Eighth Infantry Division, served at Fort Jackson, K-2 Air Base (near Taegu, South Korea), Guam, Beale Air Force Base in California and Loren Air Force Base in Maine. For his services James Alvin Bennett received the Korean Service Medal, the National Defense Service Medal, the United Nations Service Medal and the Good Conduct Medal. *Courtesy of James A. Bennett.*

James Alvin Bennett quickly learned to endure some of the primitive living conditions that marked his period of service at home and abroad. Taking care of the planes and equipment, however, was top priority. *Courtesy of James A. Bennett.*

The sound of a well-tuned plane engine on a P-80 jet fighter taking off from the K-2 Air Base at Taegu, Korea, where Bennett served. *Courtesy of James A. Bennett.*

Comfort, a smoke and some time for loafing—when one's superiors were not around—helped to make one's life bearable. The footwear that James Alvin Bennett sports is definitely not Government Issue. *Courtesy of James A. Bennett.*

A cup of Joe and a friend who listened helped to make the hard times seem less difficult. *Courtesy of James A. Bennett.*

Staff Sergeant Willis Henry Brown Jr. served in the United States Army with the Fifth Regimental Combat Team, First Cavalry Division, Service Battery of the Seventy-seventh Field Artillery Battalion. Brown participated in the siege of Outpost Harry (May 16, 1953, to June 5, 1953) when he was only nineteen years old. *Courtesy of Dot (Mrs. Willis) Brown.*

With its forward positions known as Tom, Dick and Harry, the UN troops had to endure a twenty-one-day siege at Outpost Harry. Among the several units participating for the UN forces in the siege of Outpost Harry were the Fifth Regimental Combat Team (of which Willis Henry Brown Jr. was a member), the Fifteenth Infantry Regiment and the Greek Expeditionary Forces. This siege conducted near the end of the war represented the fierce fighting that revolved around the outposts. Charles Cornell of Ohio made the print that commemorates their participation. *Courtesy of Dot (Mrs. Willis) Brown.*

The hill Outpost Harry stood upon was 185 feet high. At the time of the siege Willis Brown was only nineteen years old; he was ordered, however, to lead the men forward. During his service he suffered thirteen wounds and carried shrapnel in his back to the day of his death. For his services Staff Sergeant Willis Brown received the Purple Heart Medal, the Combat Infantryman's Badge, the Korean Service Medal with five Bronze Service Stars, the United Nations Service Medal, the National Defense Service Medal, the Good Conduct Medal and the Sharpshooter Medal for his qualifying with the machine gun. *Courtesy of Dot (Mrs. Willis) Brown.*

John C. Spangler was drafted in September of 1954 and took his basic training at Fort Jackson. He took his further training at Camp Kilmer in New Jersey. Private First Class Spangler was stationed at Zweibrucken, Germany. *Courtesy of Jerry Curtis Spangler Camp.*

John C. Spangler spent the next eighteen months transporting troops across Germany. John Spangler's wife recalled hearing John tell how he would ask each truckload of new troops if any were from North Carolina. One day to his joy he heard, "Right here!" The person was his Ellenboro friend Ken Daves. Sergeant Kenneth Daves ("K.D") served postwar in Germany; he later graduated from Appalachian State University and entered the education profession. *Courtesy of Jerry Curtis Spangler Camp.*

John C. Spangler married the former Jerry Curtis. John and Jerry had a six-month-old son Keith when John was drafted. After his discharge in 1956, John and Jerry had two daughters, Kim and Pam. *Courtesy of Jerry Curtis Spangler Camp.*

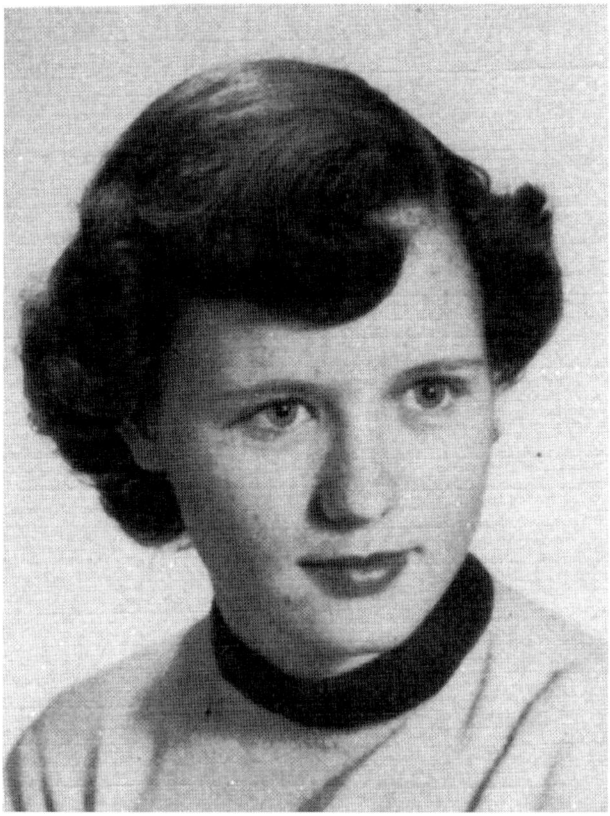

Jerry Curtis Spangler Camp, wife of John C. Spangler, was a 1953 graduate of Ellenboro High School, where she was class secretary and a member of the basketball team, glee club, annual and paper staff and commercial club. John's life was cut short in 1962 when suddenly and unexpectedly at age twenty-nine, John Spangler suffered a coronary occlusion on Christmas Eve and died. *Courtesy of Ellenboro Treasure Chest (1953) and Jerry Curtis Spangler Camp.*

Zeno Harold Daves, an uncle of Kenneth Daves whom John Spangler had mentioned, entered service on May 4, 1953, and was sent first to Camp Gordon. The new recruits were assembled, and the sergeant asked, "Who will volunteer for Korea?" Zeno, who was unmarried at the time, looked about him and saw married men and fathers; as a young, single man, he raised his hand with one other recruit. "Good!" said the officer. "You two stay here. The rest will be training for overseas." Zeno remained at Camp Gordon until his discharge on May 9, 1955. Here he receives training for his duty as military police. He attained the rank of sergeant on August 27, 1954. *Courtesy of Doris Daves.*

Sergeant Zeno Harold Daves played baseball for Ellenboro High School and even played professional ball with the American Legion. He played for the Camp Gordon baseball team. This action shot at Camp Gordon shows Zeno tagging the base before Number 10 can do so. Zeno made the play! Zeno married the former Doris Ray of Avondale in 1957. *Courtesy of Doris Daves.*

Wally Posey Melton, cousin of Ken Daves and nephew of Zeno Harold Daves, served his country, but a little later than Ken and Zeno. Airman First Class Wally Posey Melton entered the United States Air Force on April 4, 1956. He completed basic training at Lackland Air Force Base in San Antonio, Texas. Wally attended technical school at Francis E. Warren Air Force Base in Cheyenne, Wyoming. He served in French Morocco during the transitional period from colonial to self-government. Before his discharge, he became Airman of the Month. On December 15, 1962, he married Margie Wagner. *Courtesy of Wally P. Melton.*

Sergeant Ray Alfred Tessneer of Caroleen served in the United States Army as a medic. Sergeant Tessneer was in Company C, the Eighty-fifth Infantry Regiment, Tenth Infantry Division and served from 1958 to 1960. *Courtesy of Gladys B. Tessneer.*

The transportation of Sergeant Ray Alfred Tessneer included the *Marine Serpent. Courtesy of Gladys B. Tessneer.*

The Homefront and Beyond

During the Korean War, not all members of the military served in Korea. With the construction of the Iron Curtain in Europe, the United States Army and Air Force had major commitments in Central Europe. The Navy had commitments in the Mediterranean. The U.S. Marine Corps served everywhere. It was also essential for some members of the military to serve in the United States. Rutherford County had many examples of all these service personnel. The Cold War would continue for another two generations before the collapse of Russian Communism in 1989.

Civilians in the county performed important duties by encouraging the troops, working to supplement family incomes and holding families together. A tradition of service to the nation has marked Rutherford County through the years. This service began with the partisans who fought at Kings Mountain and Cowpens and continues through the War of 1812, the Mexican War, the Civil War, the Spanish-American War, World War I, World War II, Korean War, Cold War, Vietnam, Gulf War, Bosnia and the wars in Afghanistan and Iraq.

Even though the Korean War ended with the armistice of July 1953, more than fifty years later the United States still maintains more than thirty thousand troops in South Korea.

Corporal Oscar Horace Hudson served with the 547th General Dispensary attached to 116th Field Hospital in Nuremburg, Germany. *Courtesy of Oscar Horace Hudson.*

Corporal Oscar Horace Hudson worked in the dispensary in Groffenwhor from 1954–56. Hitler's SS troops had originally constructed the medical building at Groffenwhor. The sixty-bed facility had a lab, a minor surgical suite, a dental suite and x-ray facilities. *Courtesy of Oscar Horace Hudson.*

Earl E. Hennessee was a graduate of Sunshine High School and served in the U.S. Navy from 1952 until 1956. He was assigned aboard the USS *Sage* (AM-111). This minesweeper was based at Charleston, South Carolina. Hennessee served as a mechanical engineer and attained the rank of petty officer 2/C. *Courtesy of Earl E. Hennessee.*

Corporal Elbert Ray Logan, Gilkey native, entered service in April of 1953. He received training at the Third Army Food Service School at Fort Jackson, South Carolina. He served in Germany for thirteen and a half months with the Headquarters Company of the Sixty-third Tank Battalion (Germany). Corporal Elbert Ray Logan received for his services the Army Occupation Medal (Germany), the National Defense Service Medal and the Good Conduct Medal. *Courtesy of Elbert Ray Logan.*

Radioman 3/C Robert Verl Waters joined the United States Navy with Earl Hennessee, Emmett Gettys and Bud Oaks; they had basic training at Bainbridge, Maryland. Waters served six months aboard an LST at Jacksonville Navy Shipyard and three years on the USS *Tripoli* (CVE-64), a part of the Military Sea Transportation Service, a component of the Marshall Plan. *Tripoli* carried aircraft to Europe and returned with personnel and equipment. Waters crossed the Atlantic twelve times during his tour. Waters received the National Defense Service Medal, the Good Conduct Medal and the European Occupation Medal. *Courtesy of Robert Verl Waters.*

Machinist's Mate First Class Boyd Bryan Lane served aboard the USS *Cony* DDE-508. He served in the Mediterranean from May 1954 until May 1958. The *Cony* was present during the Suez crisis of 1956. Lane earned for his services the Good Conduct Medal and the National Defense Service Medal. *Courtesy of Boyd Lane.*

Private First Class Bob Bradley served in the United States Army in the 101st Airborne. *Courtesy of Bob Bradley.*

Bob Bradley recalls during basic training at Fort Jackson, South Carolina, how a young second lieutenant burned down a tent demonstrating fire safety. Fortunately the fire did not get to the barracks. *Courtesy of Bob Bradley.*

Bob Bradley was deployed to Regensburg, Germany. Here we see PFC Bradley in front of a guard post. Notice the cobblestone street. *Courtesy of Bob Bradley.*

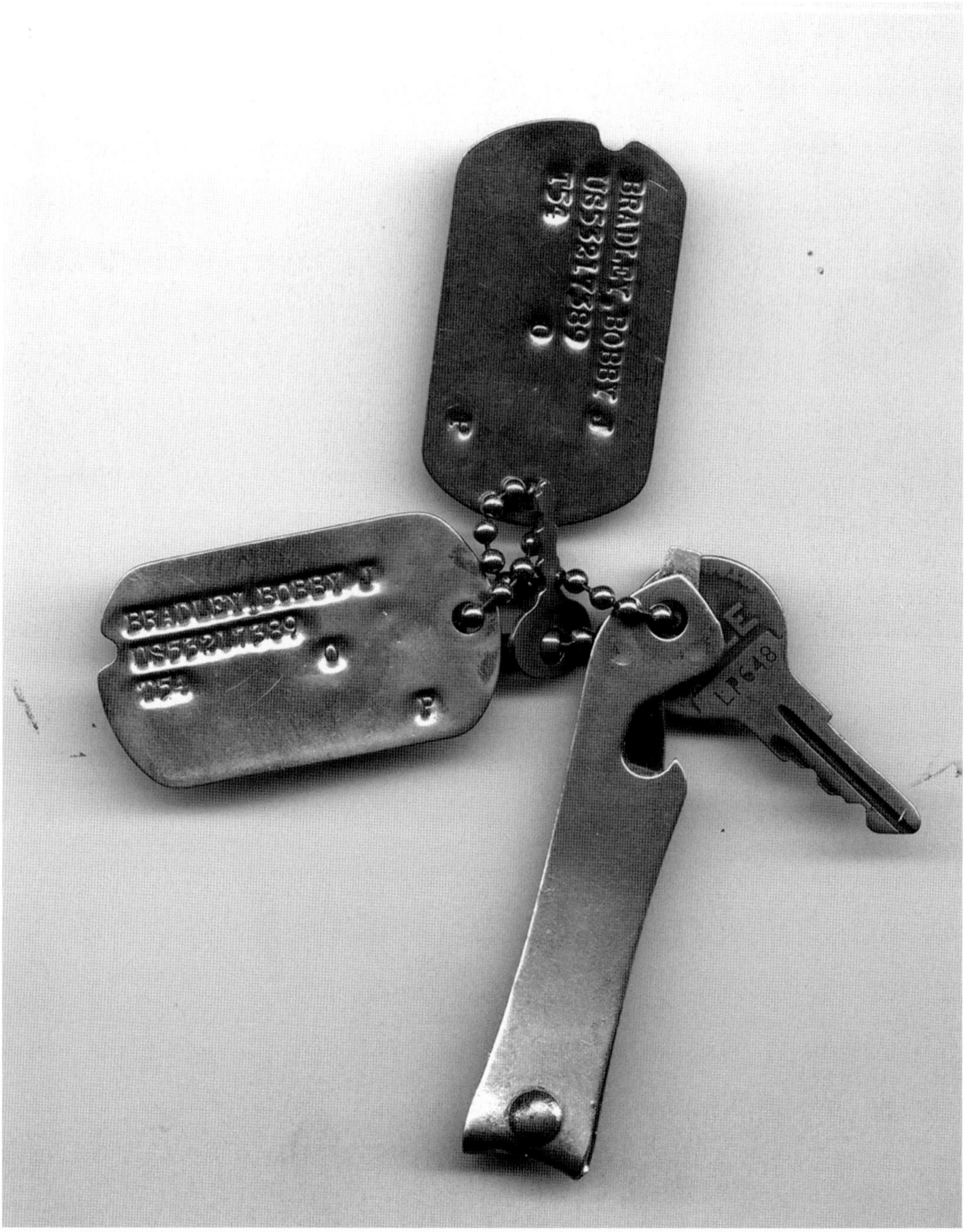

Interestingly, Bob Bradley brought with him to the interview session his dog tags. These items of identification have been in use for the past century. Bob Bradley remains active in veteran affairs. He and his wife Alice Bradley maintain their interest in veteran matters, the Rutherford County Historical Society, and the Genealogical Society of Old Tryon County; Alice is co-author with Susan Waxmunski of *Heroes of the Sixties: Lest We Forget. Courtesy of Bob Bradley.*

This photo shows a light moment as Corporal Elbert Ray Logan stands in front of a base theater showing *At War with the Army*, starring Dean Martin and Jerry Lewis. *Courtesy of Elbert Ray Logan.*

Jack Dupree Fincannon was a twenty-year veteran, serving from 1955 to 1975. He served at a wide variety of locations: Forth Jackson, South Carolina; Fort Knox, Kentucky; Fort Bragg; Alaska; Korea; Maryland; and Washington City. *Courtesy of Tamara Fincannon Robinson.*

Jack Fincannon served part of his tour with the DUKW Platoon, Service Company, Thirty-fourth Infantry Regiment, Twenty-fourth Infantry Division. *Courtesy of Tamara Fincannon Robinson.*

In 1958 Specialist Third Class Fincannon served with Headquarters Company, Third Battalion, Sixth Armored Cavalry Regiment, First Armored Division. Midway in his tour Sergeant First Class Fincannon served with the Fifteenth Military Intelligence Battalion at Fort Bragg. Fincannon retired in 1975 as a sergeant major. *Courtesy of Tamara Fincannon Robinson.*

Paul Burkley Barbee (1932–1999) entered the Army National Guard (ANGUS) on January 8, 1951. He served for four and a half years and attained the rank of sergeant before his honorable discharge on June 9, 1955. The next day (June 10, 1955) he received a direct commission as a second lieutenant with the Second Battalion HQ, 120th Infantry Regiment in Kings Mountain, North Carolina. On June 9, 1958, Barbee received a promotion to first lieutenant, Second Battle Group, 120th Infantry Staff, Hickory, North Carolina. His promotion to captain came on December 16, 1960. Barbee functioned as an assistant S-3 operations and training officer. *Courtesy of D'Etta Barbee Lasky.*

Barbee was an assistant operations officer, First Brigade, Thirtieth Infantry Division HQ. On October 8, 1965, Barbee received his promotion to major. During the next twelve years, Major Barbee was battalion executive officer with the Second Battalion. Later he assumed the role of S-3 with the Thirtieth Engineer Brigade and retained that position for the majority of his remaining career. *Courtesy of D'Etta Barbee Lasky.*

At his retirement in the fall of 1985, Barbee had the rank of lieutenant colonel. His awards include Armed Forces Reserve Medal (three times), the Army Reserve Component Achievement Award (four times), the Army Service Ribbon, the NCNG Service Award from the North Carolina National Guard (six times), the NCNG Commendation Medal (two times), the NCNG Active Duty Award, the NCNG Meritorious Service Medal, the Sharpshooter Award with a .30-caliber carbine and the Marksman with a .30-caliber carbine. During his career he had attended over thirty military school courses for professional development. *Courtesy of D'Etta Barbee Lasky.*

Not all troops were assigned to Korea. National security and the care of our troops were important also. Serving at the U.S. Navy Training Center in Bainbridge, Maryland, was Hospital Mate Third Class John Hopler Jr. Hopler was posted in Maryland for his entire period of service. Hospital Mate Third Class Hopler earned the Good Conduct Medal and the National Defense Service Medal. *Courtesy of William John Hopler.*

Private First Class Jefferson Overman "Jeff" Gettys, a Hollis native, served with M Company, Third Battalion, Sixtieth Infantry Regiment, Ninth Infantry Division. Gettys was one of five brothers to serve in the military in the 1950s. PFC Gettys entered service after two years of college at Appalachian State. A math major, he taught at both Ellenboro and East Rutherford High Schools; he also was a coach for both basketball and baseball. *Courtesy of Jeff Gettys.*

Private First Class "Jeff" Gettys was an automotive maintenance helper. Gettys served in Germany. Upon his discharge he earned the Army Occupation Medal (Germany) and the Good Conduct Medal. *Courtesy of Jeff Gettys.*

Serving in Korea for sixteen months was Private First Class Roosevelt Randolph, father of Shelly Randolph Milam. He served in the Transportation Corps and had received instruction as a stevedore and his specialty was heavy vehicle driver. *Courtesy of Shelly Randolph Milam.*

During his time in the Eighth Army, Private First Class Roosevelt Randolph guarded supply lines from ports to duty posts. Here he oversees the firing of an M-1 Garand rifle being fired by his buddy. *Courtesy of Shelly Randolph Milam.*

Jesse James McKinney served with the Psychological Warfare Detachment, 8239th AU, and was trained as a teletype operator. McKinney was located in Tokyo, Japan, at the radio studio associated with Tokyo Rose during World War II. Not only did the staff broadcast, but they also monitored radio stations in other locations. A typical broadcast would begin with "What's been happening around the world during the past seven days. Each week at this time, the voice of the United Nations Command answers that question with a comprehensive round-up of the World News in Review." *Courtesy of Jesse James McKinney and James M. Walker.*

Sandy Mush native, Keith Price (seated on right) served in the USN with the rank of lieutenant junior grade. Price received posting to Newport, Rhode Island; Athens, Georgia; Little Creek, Virginia; and Fort McClellen, Alabama. Price was selected to teach Nuclear Disaster Defense and Atomic Biological and Chemical Warfare. *Courtesy of Keith Price.*

Here Keith Price, driver, arrives in the parking place for the official car. Making sure the car is parked properly and the way is clear before exiting are important tasks as an assessor evaluates his work. *Courtesy of Keith Price.*

Keith Price (on far left) receives his commendation and promotion in an official ceremony. *Courtesy of Keith Price.*

Airman First Class Charles Butler was a great football player for Cool Springs High School. Charlie "Choo-Choo" Justice was playing for the University of North Carolina (and later the Redskins) when Butler was playing. Butler's classmates dubbed him Choo-Choo. Classmate Edward N. Washburn and Butler enlisted in 1951; they shipped first to Lackland Air Force Base and then Cheyenne, Wyoming. Charles completed his military tour in Cheyenne and returned to the county. Charles served effectively as Forest City mayor (two terms) and council member (ten years). *Courtesy of Charles Butler and Edward N. Washburn.*

Ed and Catherine Sinclair Washburn returned to Rutherford County to assume responsibility for the family businesses: Washburn Funeral Home and Washburn Store. Washburn Store, a general mercantile business, began in 1831. In regard to the store, Ed Washburn said, "If I look after the shop, it will look after me." Ed remarked to the authors that the Funeral Home was important to him and to Catherine; they felt that they were performing a service to their community. Ed's motto was, "If I do a good service, the money will take care of itself." He said he always tried not to overcharge, and they considered it important to serve their community on boards and through civic work. *Courtesy of Edward N. Washburn and James M. Walker.*

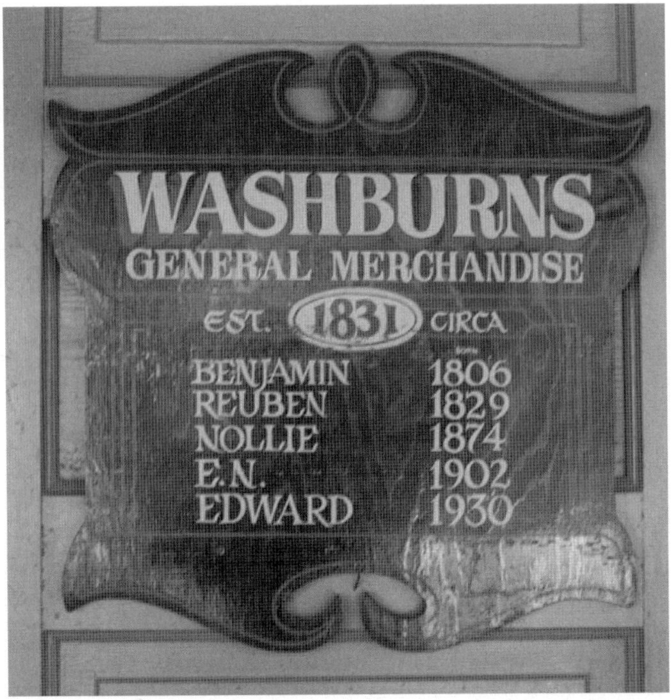

Today the Washburn House and Washburn Store and the immediate vicinity are all on the National Register of Historic Places. The store has items unavailable elsewhere. Washboards, homemade molasses, galvanized containers, lanterns, lamps, overalls and even toys of the past are on sale. *Our State* magazine, the national *DAR* magazine and UNC-TV have all featured the store. This publicity has brought customers from far and near to catch a glimpse of the past and savor the Southern hospitality of beautiful Catherine Washburn and her cordial spouse. *Courtesy of Edward N. Washburn and James M. Walker.*

Specialist Fourth Class Thomas Wayne Henderson, Company B, Seventh S&T Battalion, (FC WAKBOA) served three years in the military. His military specialty was motor transport operator. Henderson was sharpshooter with the rifle. *Courtesy of Thomas Wayne Henderson.*

Charles E. Rich joined the National Guard, completed his Electrical Fundamentals at Kessler Air Force Base in Biloxi, Mississippi, and served with the 112th Field Artillery Battalion, 30th Infantry Division. After serving in the National Guard, Rich joined the Air Force in June 1954. While at Lackland Air Force Base, he and fellow Rutherford Countians completed basic training there. *Left to right* are Charles E. Rich, Lemuel "Junior" Robbins, Frank Buff and William Whimp Hogan. Airman First Class Rich, 2nd Armament-Electronics Maintenance Squadron, 2nd Bomb Wing, 38th Air Division (SAC), provided maintenance of navigational radar for B-47 Bombers (a six-engine jet which could carry nuclear weapons) and KC-97 G ("Stratofreighter Tanker"). *Courtesy of Charles E. Rich.*

Sergeant First Class Charles E. Rich was stationed in the Azores; Sidi Slimane Air Base, French Morocco; Libya; and Turkey. After discharge from the Regular Air Force, he served three years in the Air Force Reserves. When this commitment was complete, he served with the 391st Engineers Battalion, U.S. Army Reserves and the 415th Chemical Brigade, U.S. Army. He retired April 14, 1991, after thirty years, one month and twenty-seven days and earned the National Defense Service Medal, Good Conduct Medal, Army Service Ribbon, Armed Forces Reserve Medal, Army Reserve Components Achievement Medal, two Army Commendation Medals and the Air Force Outstanding Unit Award. *Courtesy of Charles E. Rich.*

SP3 Threatha Price entered service in October of 1954. Price served as clerk with Medical Detachment 2128-1 USAH. Price served two years in service to her country. SP3 Price received an honorable discharge upon the fulfillment of her duty. Rutherford County is grateful for the dedication and service of SP3 Threatha Price Bennings and to her family and friends who forfeited her presence during her tour of duty. She is still working to enhance her country. *Courtesy of Threatha Price Bennings.*

Private First Class Evelyn Price Williams enlisted on January 21, 1953, in the Women's Army Corps, Detachment 9963rd, TSU SGO Valley Forge Army Hospital in Phoenixville, Pennsylvania. PFC Williams served one year, six months and sixteen days before her discharge on August 6, 1954. Upon her discharge, Williams received the National Defense Service Medal and the Good Conduct Medal. The authors thank her for her service to those in the military hospital and to her county. *Courtesy of Threatha Price Bennings.*

Velma Sisk (sister of Alma Frances "Fran" Sisk) and Joe Dobbins married in the 1940s. The mother of three children in the early 1950s (another one came in the late 1950s), Velma was a stay-at-home mother and devoted wife who took pride in the welfare of her family. Her husband Joe had served his country during World War II. Velma and Joe remember that in 1952 they were driving a 1950 Oldsmobile. *Courtesy of Velma and Joe Dobbins.*

Serving in their own way during the Korean War were the women at home. Alma Frances "Fran" Sisk was one of these. This photo is a favorite of her husband Albert Lancaster. She and Albert married in Marion, North Carolina, in 1941. After their marriage, she worked in the office of Florence Mills in Forest City, North Carolina, while Albert served during World War II. The 1950s found the couple busy with family: Cheryl Lynne was born June 24, 1949, and Brent Dowell was born April 17, 1952. Fran Lancaster died in 2003 after more than sixty years of marriage. Her presence is still missed. *Courtesy of Albert D. Lancaster.*

Lois Morgan (Moore), a graduate of the Alexander Schools in Union Mills, remembers the day when George A. Moore Jr. came to their home to borrow a camera. When Lois saw this U.S. Marine, she thought he was "the best looking man she had ever seen." Little did she know at that time that they would marry on March 11, 1956, after he returned from Korea. Lois had gone to work for Southern Bell after her high school graduation. She worked for Bell Telephone a total of thirty years before her retirement; her husband retired from the U.S. Marine Corps after twenty-one and a half years. *Courtesy of Lois Morgan Moore.*

Lois Elaine Hudson enlisted in the military in North Platte, Nebraska, and served during World War II as a Pharmacist's Mate Second Class. She received the Honorable Service Lapel Button upon her discharge from the U.S. Naval Auxiliary Air Station, Waldron Field, Corpus Christi, Texas. Lois Hudson married Ross Hudson, well-known athlete and model citizen from Forest City. Fortunately for the county, this civic-minded young woman and her husband made their home in the county. *Courtesy of Lois Hudson.*

Robert Benjamin Thompson was in the United States Army during World War II and suffered wounds in the Battle of the Bulge at age nineteen. After the war, he received his U.S. Army Commission at Presbyterian College in Clinton, South Carolina, and met Rebecca Jane Harrill from Rutherford County. They married on July 31, 1948, and he began work as a Duke Power chemist in Salisbury, North Carolina. Jane Thompson (Gurley) was born in 1950. Thompson was recalled into active service during the Korean War; he trained Fort Benning, Georgia, soldiers going to Korea. Jane and her mother relocated to Rutherford County until Thompson was able to secure an apartment for them on post. After his discharge, the family moved back to Salisbury, where Thompson continued his work with Duke Power, working for thirty-six and a half years as a chemist and plant engineer. During the last part of his career, Thompson was in charge of all the coal-fire steam production plants. His claim to Rutherford County is meeting and marrying Rebecca Jane Harrill. Robert Benjamin Thompson celebrated his eightieth birthday on January 12, 2006. *Courtesy of Robert Benjamin Thompson, Rebecca Jane Harrill Thompson and Jane Thompson Gurley.*

Even as this is written, members of the 505th Engineer Battalion of the North Carolina National Guard are on active duty in Iraq. The 505th Engineer Battalion includes more than 350 soldiers from North Carolina. The members from Forest City are Specialist George Miller, Specialist Duane Mote, Specialist David Putnam, Sergeant Von Littlejohn, Sergeant Keith Carpenter, Staff Sergeant Michael Lail, Staff Sergeant Robert Lail, Sergeant Jose Lopez, Sergeant Randy Hicks and Private First Class Michael Reynolds. The members from Bostic include Sergeant Sean Bibler and Sergeant T. Bryson Sane. The member from Cane Creek is Sergeant John Street. *Courtesy of Doris and Carl Harris.*

Representing those now serving is Sergeant T. Bryson Sane, standing in front of the Hobart Daniel Armory. This twenty-two-year-old soldier from the Washburn community is married to the former Cindal Harrelson; Bryson is the great-grandson of World War II veteran John T. Harris. Sergeant Sane attended East Rutherford High School and Isothermal Community College. He spent about a year after September 11 guarding the National Security Agency. His parents are Mark and Yvonne Haulk of Forest City. His grandparents are Steve Sane and Barbara Sane of Green Hill, Carl and Doris Harris of Forest City and Robert Maurice Sane and Irene Sane, also of Green Hill. *Courtesy of Doris and Carl Harris.*

The Rutherford County Honor Guard, formed in the fall of 2004, is an effort to honor service personnel at their final resting place. Men and women of all branches of service render final military honors to those who serve. Family members of any service personnel can request the services of the Honor Guard at the final rites. Pictured here and standing at attention are some of the members of the Rutherford County Honor Guard in November 2004. *Courtesy of James M. Walker.*

From 1950 to 1953 the United States had joined United Nations forces to protest the threat to democracy. Those who served during the Korean War could never forget. More than forty years after the Korean War, the Korean War Veterans Memorial honored those who answered the call, who worked and fought, and who gave their lives for their country. On July 27, 1995, the dedication ceremonies, with President William Jefferson Clinton as a keynote speaker, at last celebrated the Korean War veterans: dead, alive and missing in action. *Courtesy of Danielle Watson.*

Bibliography

Davis, Anita P. *Real Heroes: Rutherford County Men Who Made the Supreme Sacrifice During World War II.* Spartanburg, SC: Honoribus Press, 2002.

Davis, Anita P., and James M. Walker. *Forest City*. Mt. Pleasant, SC: Arcadia Publishing Company, 2006.

———. *Rutherford County in World War II: Volume I.* Mt. Pleasant, SC: Arcadia Publishing Company, 2003.

———. *Rutherford County in World War II: Volume II.* Mt. Pleasant, SC: Arcadia Publishing Company, 2004.

Gastonia Gazette article from Ray Humphries.

Gillespie, Bailey, and Joy Gillespie. *Korean War Remembered.* Spindale, NC: POW Book, 1998.

Hastings, Max. *Korea.* New York: Simon and Schuster, 1988.

McConnell, Malcolm. "Johnson's List." *Reader's Digest*, January 1997.

Treasure Chest. Ellenboro High School Yearbook, 1950.

Treasure Chest. Ellenboro High School Yearbook, 1953.

U.S. Army Center of Military History. "Korean War Medal of Honor Recipients." http://www.army.mil/cmh-pg/mohkor2.htm.

U.S. Soldiers' and Airmen's Home Newspaper. July 24, 1998.

Waxmunski, Susan and Alice Bradley. *Heroes of the Sixties: Lest We Forget.* Forest City, NC: Genealogical Society of Old Tryon County, 2004.

Index

C

D

E

F

G